PHONICS
Practice Book

Intermediate

Orlando   Boston   Dallas   Chicago   San Diego

Visit *The Learning Site!*
www.harcourtschool.com

ISBN 0-15-315213-3

1 2 3 4 5 6 7 8 9 10   073   02 01 00 99

CONTENTS

Harcourt Brace School Publishers

Unit 3: More Work with Vowels

Phonics Practice Book

Harcourt Brace School Publishers

Unit 4: More Work with Consonants

Unit 5: Digraphs

Unit 6: Contractions and Possessives

Unit 7: Inflected Endings

Phonics Practice Book

Harcourt Brace School Publishers

Unit 8: Prefixes, Suffixes, and Agents

Cut-Out Fold-Up Books

Circle the letter or letters that stand for the beginning sound. Then write the letter or letters to complete the word.

1
k
b
t

_____ear

2
c
w
p

_____ar

3
d
g
r

_____oad

4
z
p
s

_____ig

5
w
f
x

_____ater

6
m
l
g

_____irl

7
t
p
h

_____at

8
j
k
n

_____ar

9
z
h
v

_____ebra

10
p
y
l

_____arn

11
f
b
m

_____ish

12
b
g
r

_____opc

13
br
qu
cl

_____een

14
b
x
l

_____oy

15
p
k
d

_____ite

Name _____

Say the name of each picture. Circle the letter or letters that stand for the beginning sound. Then write the letter or letters to complete the word.

1	2	3
p v s _____an	s b t _____op	l f s _____un

4	5	6
m n qu _____ouse	p l z _____og	n p k _____ie

7	8	9
t n s _____ail	d p v _____og	p qu h _____ilt

10	11	12
r f z _____ox	g m p _____ate	k l j _____am

13	14	15
m b n _____oon	l k y _____ey	t p h _____at

Initial Consonants

Phonics Practice Book

Harcourt Brace School Publishers

Name _____

Circle the word that names each picture. Then write the word on the line.

1	van / man / tan	2	mix / six / fix	3	boat / goat / coat
4	mat / cat / hat	5	nut / hut / but	6	mean / queen / lean
7	gap / map / lap	8	pig / big / wig	9	red / bed / fed
10	fan / man / can	11	sock / lock / dock	12	run / fun / sun
13	hot / cot / lot	14	bib / rib / fib	15	met / jet / pet

Harcourt Brace School Publishers

Phonics Practice Book

Initial Consonants

9

Name _____

1. I will be _____ years old on my next birthday.

       pen   bin   ten

2. John brought his _____ to the baseball game.

       hot   bat   cob

3. The spider made a _____ in the corner.

       web   rob   bib

4. She used a _____ to write the letter.

       hen   pen   tin

5. I hammered a _____ into the wall.

       pail   sail   nail

6. John wiped his feet on the _____.

       pat   sat   mat

7. The _____ hid in a hole.

       box   fox   wax

8. Dad opened the _____ of jelly.

       car   far   jar

9. Pam took a nap on a _____.

       dot   cot   hot

10. The cat hit the ball of _____.

       barn   yarn   park

Harcourt Brace School Publishers

Write the answer to each clue.

1. You use me to pick up leaves.

   My name rhymes with *bake*.

   _____

2. You wear us on your feet.

   Our name rhymes with *rocks*.

   _____

3. I am a farm animal,

   and my name rhymes with *jig*.

   _____

4. I wear a crown, and

   my name rhymes with *seen*.

   _____

5. I am a place to keep money.

   My name rhymes with *tank*.

   _____

6. I shine in the sky at night.

   My name rhymes with *soon*.

   _____

7. You do this to a soccer ball.

   It rhymes with *wick*.

   _____

8. You use me when you eat.

   My name rhymes with *cork*.

   _____

9. This is how snow feels.

   It rhymes with *hold*.

   _____

10. Seven days make one of me.

    My name rhymes with *peek*.

    _____

Name _____

b	d	h	m	p	s	w
c	f	l	n	r	v	z

1. Our class took a bus trip to the _____oo last _____eek.

2. We took bag _____unches and had a _____icnic.

3. We saw a polar _____ear and a _____ion.

4. A _____onkey was hanging from a _____imb.

5. The _____ox was hiding in a _____ole.

6. We took a break on a _____ench under a tree.

7. We drank glasses of _____old _____ater.

8. There were _____any kinds of _____eer.

9. We saw a _____ed _____ird in a tree.

10. We _____isited the _____eptile house.

11. We snacked on _____elon and _____ananas.

12. A train took us to see the _____enguins.

13. The afternoon _____un was very _____ot.

14. We left the zoo at _____our o'clock.

15. I took a _____ap on the bus ride _____ome.

Harcourt Brace School Publishers

Name _____

1.
x
s
ff

2.
l
t
r

3.
p
f
n

4.
r
d
l

5.
m
ll
zz

6.
mb
n
t

7.
k
p
b

8.
d
k
t

9.
n
m
f

10.
p
g
s

11.
k
ff
x

12.
gg
ss
k

13.
k
x
m

14.
d
p
b

15.
b
d
n

Harcourt Brace School Publishers

Circle the word that names each picture. Then write the word.

1	map man mad	2	can cat cab	3	bin bat bib
4	lip lit lid	5	leak leaf lead	6	six sit sip
7	mill mitt mix mitt	8	cup cut cub	9	well web wet
10	put pan pig	11	lamb lad lap	12	click clip cliff
13	dot dog doll	14	bead bean beak	15	jab jazz jam

Harcourt Brace School Publishers

Final Consonants

Phonics Practice Book

Name _____

Circle the answer to each clue. Write the word.

1. I am another name for *test*. _____

    quit   queen   quiz

2. I am part of your mouth. _____

    lip   lid   like

3. I am on the side of a mountain. _____

    clap   cliff   clip

4. I am between five and seven. _____

    sat   sit   six

5. I am another name for *lawn*. _____

    grab   grass   glue

6. I am something you can put on bread. _____

    jam   jar   pan

7. I am a game you can play. _____

    ten   tag   tap

8. I am where you go to learn. _____

    look   pick   school

9. I am a baby sheep. _____

    lamp   lamb   cat

10. I am the sound a bee makes. _____

    buzz   bun   bud

11. I come out when the sun sets. _____

    mood   mop   moon

12. I am part of a sandwich. _____

    broom   bread   beat

Name _____

Say the name of each picture. Circle the word, and then write it.

1	bat / bad / bag	2	cat / cab / can	3	pad / pan / pat
4	gun / gum / got	5	tub / tug / tap	6	end / ever / egg
7	sub / sun / sum	8	cob / cap / cot	9	leaf / lead / leak
10	bat / bar / ball	11	mate / mat / map	12	bud / bus / but
13	rug / run / rub	14	bet / bed / beg	15	mill / mix / mitt

Harcourt Brace School Publishers

16 Final Consonants   Phonics Practice Book

Name _____

1		○ We used the mat to wipe our feet.
		○ We used a map to find the gold.
		○ We were mad about the game.
2		○ Mrs. Jones rode a bike to work.
		○ Mrs. Jones drove a cart to work.
		○ Mrs. Jones took a cab to work.
3		○ Dad put a lid on the pot.
		○ Dad put a light in the garage.
		○ Dad lit the wood for the fire.
4		○ I will lead the band.
		○ The sink has a leak.
		○ The leaf fell off the tree.
5		○ Ann and Kay had a cup of tea.
		○ Ann cut her knee today.
		○ Ann and Kay saw a cub.
6		○ Jan drew a dot on the paper.
		○ Jan has a pet dog.
		○ Jan has a paper doll.
7		○ The bird has a bead necklace.
		○ The bird ate beans for lunch.
		○ The bird has a big beak.
8		○ Dan stood on the cliff.
		○ Dan put the clip on the papers.
		○ Dan can click his fingers.

Use letters below to complete the sentences in the story. You may use some letters more than once.

p   m   k   d   n   g   t   x   w

The Jones family wen___ to a far___ near their tow___. Don and Pat helped fee___ the chickens, the pigs, and the co___. Dad saw a ma___ mil___ the co___. Mom gathered eggs from the he___.

Mom and Pat made ja___ in a pa___. Don saw a little chic___ in a bo___. Dad picked cor___ in the garde___.

For lunch, the Jones family ate corn, ha___, sala___, and warm bread with honey. They had ice crea___ for dessert. Then Pat and Don played ta___ in the yar___. Mom read a boo___ while Dad took a na___.

Say the name of each picture. Write the letter that stands for the sound you hear in the middle of the word.

1 ti___er	2 ca___in	3 spi___er
4 ru___er	5 ca___el	6 pea___ut
7 pa___er	8 sa___ad	9 wa___on
10 mo___ey	11 mu___ic	12 ba___y
13 le___on	14 wa___er	15 me___er
16 co___or	17 de___ert	18 pia___o

Write the word that answers each clue. You will not use all the words.

melon	desert	tulip	honey	wagon	baby
spider	paper	money	tiger	sweater	robin
camel	water	ruler	music	dragon	tuba

1. You can buy things with me. _____

2. You can draw on me. _____

3. I am a fruit you can eat. _____

4. I make a web. _____

5. I taste very sweet. _____

6. You can ride in me. _____

7. Put me on when you are cold. _____

8. I help you draw a straight line. _____

9. You hear me on the radio. _____

10. My nest is in a tree. _____

11. Drink me when you are thirsty. _____

12. I am a make-believe animal. _____

13. You can see me in a band. _____

14. I grow in the spring. _____

15. I am a hot, dry place that gets little rain. _____

Harcourt Brace School Publishers

Fill in the circle next to the sentence that tells about each picture.

1

- ○ Dad took Betsy to the zoo.
- ○ Dad took the dragon to the zoo.
- ○ Dad took the robin to the zoo.

2

- ○ Dad found a spiderweb in the corner.
- ○ Dad found a beaver in the corner.
- ○ The spiderweb was on the tiger.

3

- ○ The camel swam in the river.
- ○ They saw a camel in the desert.
- ○ They rode a camel around the park.

4

- ○ Dad and Betsy made some money.
- ○ Dad and Betsy listened to some music.
- ○ Dad and Betsy were in a band.

5

- ○ Salad is good for lunch.
- ○ A woman was on the bench.
- ○ They ate melon on the bench.

6

- ○ Betsy poured a glass of juice.
- ○ A robin splashed in the water.
- ○ Dad helped Betsy get some water.

Name _____

1	2	3	4
__o__	__u__i__	__u__	__e__

5	6	7	8
__e__	__i__	__o__	__o__a__

9	10	11	12
__u__	__a__	__ea__e__	__o__

13	14	15	16
__a__e__	__a__	__ea__	__u__

Name _____

Use the letters below to complete the sentences. You may use some letters more than once.

l b t n p h g w f r d m

The Nolen __amily went to their ca__in near the lake. They __ulled their things up the steep __ill in a wa__on. Dad unlocked the doo__, and they all went inside. Dad saw a spi__er web by the __indow.

Carol and Judy walked down to the __ake. They ate some pea__uts. The __irls saw a __oman with __our children in a sai__ boa__ on the wa__er.

Later that __ay, the Nolen family ate sa__ad and ha__ for supper. They each had a slice of me__on. Then Mark played the pia__o. Everyone was happy after the __ong day.

Write the answers to the questions.

1. Where did the Nolen family take a trip to?_____

_____

2. What did the girls see at the lake? _____

_____

Fill in the circle next to the word that names the picture.

1
- ◯ wet
- ◯ wed
- ◯ web

2
- ◯ cob
- ◯ cot
- ◯ cod

3
- ◯ bed
- ◯ bet
- ◯ beg

4
- ◯ dot
- ◯ dog
- ◯ doll

5
- ◯ top
- ◯ mop
- ◯ hop

6
- ◯ lean
- ◯ leap
- ◯ leaf

7
- ◯ camel
- ◯ cable
- ◯ cattle

8
- ◯ sum
- ◯ gum
- ◯ hum

9
- ◯ hut
- ◯ hat
- ◯ hit

10
- ◯ bell
- ◯ sell
- ◯ well

11
- ◯ box
- ◯ fox
- ◯ wax

12
- ◯ bus
- ◯ bun
- ◯ bud

13
- ◯ bin
- ◯ pin
- ◯ tin

14
- ◯ cut
- ◯ nut
- ◯ rut

15
- ◯ cab
- ◯ cart
- ◯ cat

Harcourt Brace School Publishers

Test of Initial, Final, and Medial Consonants

Phonics Practice Book

Name _____

Fill in the circle next to the sentence that best tells about each picture.

1		○ Uncle Mac saw a cat at the zoo.
		○ Uncle Mac saw a zebra at the zoo.
		○ Uncle Mac saw a seal at the zoo.
2		○ Pat and Sam saw a crab at the beach.
		○ Pat and Sam saw a crow at the beach.
		○ Pat and Sam saw a crown at the beach.
3		○ Dan and his mother took cookies to the party.
		○ Dan helped his mother play music.
		○ Dan helped his mother toss the salad.
4		○ Dad poured Ann a glass of milk.
		○ Dad made Ann a sandwich.
		○ Dad gave Ann some melon.
5		○ Grandmother baked a cake for Kate.
		○ Grandmother made a quilt for Kate.
		○ Grandmother fixed the bike for Kate.
6		○ The chicken ate a seed.
		○ The chicken ran across the yard.
		○ The chicken laid an egg.
7		○ We rode the cart down the hill.
		○ We rode the sled down the hill.
		○ We rode the wagon down the hill.
8		○ We like to play in the water on a warm day.
		○ We like to play in the sand on a warm day.
		○ We like to play in the cabin on a warm day.

Name _____

m**a**t

b**a**t

If a word has only one vowel, and it comes between two consonants, the vowel is usually short. Write *a* to complete each word that has the short *a* sound.

1	p ___ n	2	p ___ n	3	fl ___ g
4	c ___ t	5	h ___ m	6	c ___ t
7	m ___ n	8	pl ___ nt	9	b ___ d
10	p ___ t	11	h ___ t	12	b ___ g
13	m ___ p	14	b ___ g	15	p ___ nts
16	f ___ n	17	p ___ g	18	tr ___ cks

Short Vowel: /a/a

Phonics Practice Book

Name _____

1.
pod
paid
pad

_____

2.
hat
hit
hate

_____

3.
pane
pan
pain

_____

4.
cap
cape
cup

_____

5.
fine
fun
fan

_____

6.
cane
cub
can

_____

7.
meat
mat
mate

_____

8.
tack
take
tuck

_____

9.
but
bat
bait

_____

10.
cape
cat
cot

_____

11.
rug
rage
rag

_____

12.
pans
pants
paints

_____

Short Vowel: /a/a

27

Write a word that rhymes with each picture name.

1 cap 	2 pad 	3 bat 
_____	_____	_____
4 lamp 	5 fan 	6 ham 
_____	_____	_____
7 tag 	8 tack 	9 ax 
_____	_____	_____
10 pan 	11 map 	12 hand
_____	_____	_____

Name _____

Write the word from the box that completes each sentence. You will not use all the words.

> bat   pan   bait
> bag   pain   cap

1. Jack has his _____ .

2. Put the lid on the _____ .

3. Pam hands the _____ to Joan.

4. Dan has a _____ of apples for Ann.

> tuck   pad   tack
> mate   hat   mat

5. I wipe my feet on the _____ .

6. My _____ keeps my ears warm.

7. Mary writes her name on the _____ .

8. Kim uses a _____ to hang her ribbon.

Read the story and answer the questions.

The Picnic

Last summer the Frank family went on a picnic by a lake. Dad and Zack played in the water. Mom and Brad floated on a raft. Patty played in the sand.

They found a shady place to eat. They had ham, yams, and cans of juice. After lunch Zack and Brad took a nap.

Dad, Mom, and Patty played tag. They saw something black running in the grass. Patty tried to catch it. She tripped and fell. The fast black cat ran from her hands. The cat woke Zack and Brad from their naps.

The Franks went down to the lake. They saw tadpoles in the water. Then they drove home in their van.

1. What did the Franks do for fun on their picnic? _____

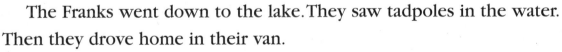

2. What did the Franks eat for lunch?

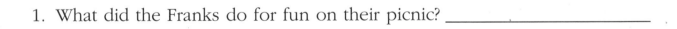

3. Why did Patty fall?

_____

Harcourt Brace School Publishers

bed

If a word has only one vowel, and it comes between two consonants, the vowel is usually short. Write *e* to complete each word that has the short *e* sound.

1 p___g	**2** b___t	**3** p___n
4 b___x	**5** w___b	**6** f___nce
7 ch___ck	**8** s___n	**9** t___n
10 sh___ll	**11** d___g	**12** d___sk
13 h___n	**14** v___n	**15** v___st
16 n___ck	**17** b___lt	**18** c___p

Circle the name of each picture. Then write the word.

1
pear
pen
pet

2
bet
bead
bed

3
net
neat
near

4
cheap
check
cheek

5
teen
tent
ten

6
shall
shell
shut

7
steep
stop
step

8
well
wheel
will

9
bunch
beach
bench

10
teen
tint
tent

11
wet
wheat
with

12
jet
jack
jab

Short Vowel: /e/e • Reading Words with Short e

Write a word that rhymes with the name of each picture.

1 bed	2 tent	3 pen
_____	_____	_____
4 bell	5 egg	6 men
_____	_____	_____
7 vest	8 well	9 leg
_____	_____	_____
10 bench	11 dress	12 hen
_____	_____	_____

Look at the pictures above. Do what the sentences tell you.

1. Draw a pet on the bed.

2. Draw more men.

3. Draw a fence next to the tent.

4. Draw a bow on the vest.

5. Draw a hen by the pen.

6. Draw a pet with four legs.

7. Draw a jet over the well.

8. Draw one more hen.

9. Draw a nest under the egg.

10. Draw a belt on the dress.

Short Vowel: /e/e   **33**

Name _____

Write the word that completes each sentence. You will not use all the words.

Red	pen	put	pet	fed

1. Jeff got a dog for a _____ .

2. Jeff said, "I will call you _____ ."

3. Jeff _____ his dog a snack.

4. Jeff made a _____ for Red in the yard.

bed	Teen	beg	Ten	led

5. Jeff showed Red how to _____ .

6. Jeff _____ Red on a short walk.

7. Jeff made a _____ for Red.

8. Jeff said, "_____ o'clock. Time for bed."

34

Short Vowel: /e/ e • Reading Words with Short e

Phonics Practice Book

Harcourt Brace School Publishers

Read the poem. Then write the answers to the questions.

Ned and Ted's Hike

Ned went for a hike with Ted,

Up and down where the path led.

They saw a spider in a web,

And a boy whose name was Jeb.

They saw a red bird in a nest,

And a girl called Jen in a vest.

They saw a bug with six black legs

And a hen with lots of eggs.

They saw a fox outside its den,

And some rabbits in a pen.

Then Ned and Ted went home to rest

And tell Aunt Meg what they liked best.

1. What did Ned and Ted see on their hike?_____

_____

_____

_____

2. What did Ned and Ted plan to do when they got home?

_____

Now circle all the words in the poem that have the short *e* sound.

Name _____

Write the word that names the picture.

1	2	3
4	5	6
7	8	9
10	11	12
13	14	15

Harcourt Brace School Publishers

Review: Short *a* and *e*

Phonics Practice Book

Name _____

Write the word that answers each clue. You will not use all of the words.

jam   ten   pan   pen   cap   cup   cab   bed   tan

1. You can ride in it. _____

2. We eat it on bread. _____

3. It comes after nine. _____

4. You can write with it. _____

5. You wear it on your head. _____

6. You can sleep in it. _____

bet   smell   stem   bat   red   stream   fast   bell   reed

7. You hit a ball with it. _____

8. You hold this part of a flower. _____

9. It tells how some people run. _____

10. It is a color in the American flag. _____

11. You hear it ring. _____

12. You do this with your nose. _____

mitt

If a word has only one vowel and it comes between two consonants, the vowel is usually short. Write *i* to complete each picture name that has the short *i* sound.

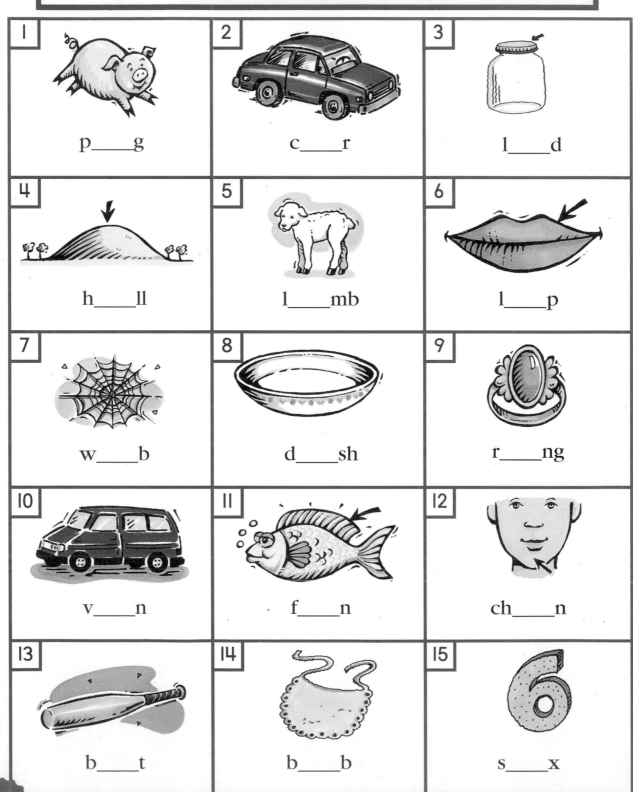

1 p____g

2 c____r

3 l____d

4 h____ll

5 l____mb

6 l____p

7 w____b

8 d____sh

9 r____ng

10 v____n

11 f____n

12 ch____n

13 b____t

14 b____b

15 s____x

Harcourt Brace School Publishers

Write *yes* or *no* to answer each question.

1		Is the baby wearing a bib? _____
2		Did Kip see six pigs at the farm? _____
3		Did Kim hit the ball? _____
4		Do fish swim in a pond? _____
5		Did Jim have his mitt? _____
6		Can a tree have a limb? _____
7		Is Mindy with the other kids? _____
8		Does the wig fit on Ginny's head? _____
9		Did the dog dig the hole? _____
10		Are the pins in the bin? _____

Name _____

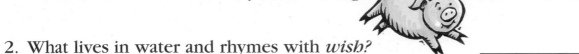

1. What lives on a farm and rhymes with *big?* _____

2. What lives in water and rhymes with *wish?* _____

3. What do you drink that rhymes with *silk?* _____

4. What goes on your head and rhymes with *pig?* _____

5. What comes after five and rhymes with *mix?* _____

6. What goes on a pan and rhymes with *kid?* _____

7. What part of your mouth rhymes with *dip?* _____

8. What part of a fish rhymes with *win?* _____

9. What can you walk to the top of that rhymes with *fill?* _____

10. What part of your body rhymes with *tip?* _____

11. What is the opposite of *small* and rhymes with *dig?* _____

12. What names a color and rhymes with *sink?* _____

13. What fits on your finger and rhymes with *king?* _____

14. What do you put food on? It rhymes with *fish.* _____

15. What sound does a clock make? It rhymes with *lick.* _____

Harcourt Brace School Publishers

Write the word that completes each sentence. You will not use all the words.

limb	sit	hill	with	mitt
tip	lip	hit	Bill	win

1

Will went up a _____.

2

He took his ball and

_____.

3

At the top of the hill, Will met

_____.

4

He sat on a _____ in

a tree.

5

"Now we can play

_____ my baseball,"

said Will.

6

Bill _____ the ball.

7

"You _____!" said

Will.

Read the story and answer the questions.

A TRIP TO THE BEACH

Jim and Jill went to the beach with their family. "We will sit here," said Mother. Jim and Jill began to dig in the sand. They made a big hill.

Jim and Jill saw six fish swim by. The fish had pretty red fins. "I wish I could swim like a fish," said Jill.

"You can sit here and dip your feet in," said Mother. Jill put the tip of her big toe in the water. "It is cold!" she said.

Baby Liz came to sit with Jim and Jill. Liz wore a pink bib. Jim scooped up some water and let it drip on her toes. That made Liz grin.

"It is almost six o'clock," said Mother. "It is time to go home for dinner."

1. Who took a trip to the beach? _____

2. What did Jim and Jill do in the sand? _____

3. Why did the family have to go home? _____

_____

Now underline all the short *i* words in the story.

Harcourt Brace School Publishers

Name _____

If a word has only one vowel and it comes between two consonants, the vowel is usually short. Write *o* to complete each picture name that has the short *o* sound.

t<u>o</u>p

1 f___x	2 h___t	3 d___ll
4 s___ck	5 w___b	6 r___ck
7 j___r	8 m___p	9 p___n
10 l___g	11 b___x	12 h___ll
13 h___n	14 p___t	15 cl___ck

Short Vowel: /o/*o*

Name _____

Write *yes* or *no* to answer each question.

1		1. Can a fox sit on a rock? _____
2		2. Did Ross catch a cod with his fishing rod? _____
3		3. Could Rob buy a top at the toy shop? _____
4		4. Did Jan put her doll on the cot? _____
5		5. Does Tom sell boxes at his job? _____
6		6. Did Donna drop her box? _____
7		7. Is the pot on top of the stove? _____
8		8. Did the pot get hot? _____
9		9. Does this sign tell you to stop? _____
10		10. Is Bob taller than the clock? _____

Short Vowel: /o/*o*

Write a word that rhymes with each picture name.

1 rock	2 box	3 cot
4 top	5 cob	6 log
7 pond	8 sock	9 rod
10 clock	11 ox	12 pot

Short Vowel: /o/o • Phonograms   **45**

Write the word that completes each sentence. You will not use all the words.

mop	cob	hot	Jon	mom
pot	lock	stop	box	got

1. Jon went camping with his

_____.

2. Jon got wood out of a

_____.

3. His mom built a _____

fire.

4. Jon _____ out a pot and

put water in it.

5. He set the _____ over the

fire to get hot.

6. Then he added the corn on the

_____.

7. Soon _____ called, "Mom, I

think the corn is hot."

8. It was hard to _____

eating that corn!

Harcourt Brace School Publishers

Name _____

The Top of the World

A frog hopped out of the pond. He hopped along, through the fog. The frog saw a dog on top of a rock. "What are you looking for?" asked the frog.

"I want to see the top of the world," said the dog.

The frog hopped on, into the bog. He saw a fox on a log. "What are you looking for?" asked the frog.

"I want to see the top of the world," said the fox.

The frog hopped on through the fog. He saw a bird on a limb. "What are you looking for?" asked the frog.

"I want to see the top of the world," said the bird.

The frog hopped to a spot on the dock. Then the sun came out and the fog went away. The frog saw the cool water and the blue sky. He felt the hot sun on his back. "This must be the top of the world," he said. Then he hopped back into the pond.

1. Who did the frog see as he hopped along?

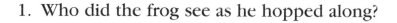

_____

2. What did the dog, fox, and bird want to see?

_____

3. What made the frog think he had found the top of the world?

_____

_____

Name _____

Circle the letter that stands for the short vowel sound in each picture name.

1. a
   e
   o

2. e
   o
   i

3. i
   o
   a

4. e
   o
   i

5. o
   e
   i

6. a
   i
   o

7. i
   o
   e

8. o
   i
   a

9. a
   i
   e

10. o
    e
    i

11. i
    o
    a

12. i
    a
    o

13. e
    i
    o

14. a
    o
    i

15. i
    o
    e

Harcourt Brace School Publishers

Name _____

Circle the answer to each clue. Then write the word on the line.

1. It is part of your mouth. _____

   lip   lap   leap

2. You put this on your foot. _____

   sack   sock   sick

3. You need a key to open this. _____

   lake   lock   lick

4. This animal lives on a farm. _____

   pig   peg   pain

5. When you go camping, you sleep on this. _____

   cot   cat   cut

6. A baby wears this. _____

   bob   bib   bud

7. You hold this when you go fishing. _____

   rid   red   rod

8. You use a shovel to do this. _____

   dog   dig   dime

9. You can climb to the top of this. _____

   hall   heel   hill

10. This animal hops and likes the water. _____

   frog   flip   float

Name _____

mug   The letter *u* often stands for the short *u* sound. Sometimes the letters *ou* stand for the short *u*

Country   sound. Write the word that names each picture.

cub   mug   rug   cuff   duck   tub   bus   bug

1. _____

2. _____

3. _____

4. _____

5. _____

6. _____

7. _____

8. _____

Write the word that completes each sentence.
You will not use all the words.

young   stump   rough   stamp   earth   country

9. We sat on a tree _____ .

10. A kitten is a _____ cat.

11. The _____ waves rocked our boat.

12. The United States is the _____ we live in.

The words below are hidden in the puzzle. Some words go across. Some words go down. Find and circle each one.

tub pump duck truck drum tough gum
thumb puppy rough sun cousin bug rust double

r	o	u	g	h	c	p	h	d	e	d	m	p
u	a	x	u	t	z	t	u	b	b	o	g	u
s	u	n	m	e	t	h	d	l	p	u	m	p
t	d	r	b	c	o	u	s	i	n	b	f	p
b	r	j	o	k	u	m	a	u	i	l	j	y
d	u	c	k	f	g	b	u	g	c	e	i	w
q	m	n	h	s	h	g	t	r	u	c	k	v

Write the name of each picture.

Write the word that completes each sentence. You will not use all the words.

Sue   bus   plum   bump   duck
trip   cousin   Gus   snow   under   lunch

1 _____ went to school.

2 He rode on a big _____ with many other children.

3 Gus saw a _____ swimming in a pond.

4 The bus went over a _____ in the road.

5 At school, Gus saw his _____.

6 They sat _____ a tree to eat.

7 Gus had some juice with his _____ .

8 He pulled out a ripe, purple _____ .

Name _____

1. What covers the floor and rhymes with *mug*? _____

2. What has a shell and rhymes with *cut*? _____

3. What shines in the sky and rhymes with *fun*? _____

4. What makes a good pet and rhymes with *guppy*? _____

5. What says "quack" and rhymes with *luck*? _____

6. What has six legs and rhymes with *jug*? _____

7. What is a part of your hand and rhymes with *crumb*? _____

8. What can you drink from that rhymes with *bug*? _____

9. What means "two" and rhymes with *trouble*? _____

10. What is the opposite of smooth and rhymes with *tough*? _____

Read the story, and answer the questions.

Buff, the bear cub, went for a walk in the woods to look for bugs. He saw a duck in a pond, but he did not find any bugs. He saw bright red berries, but he did not find any bugs. He saw nuts on a tree, but he did not find any bugs. He saw a gull in the sky, but he did not find any bugs.

Buff walked on. A big buck jumped across the path. Then Buff walked in the mud and came to an old hut.

Buff rubbed his back against a tree stump. The bark felt rough on his back. Then Buff rolled down a hill, thumping and bumping until he hit a rock.

When Buff got up, he saw bugs under the rock. He dug up the bugs and ate them. There were just enough. Then Buff curled up and took a nap.

1. Why did Buff go for a walk?

_____

2. What did Buff see while he was looking for bugs?

_____

_____

3. How did Buff find the bugs?

_____

4. What did Buff do after he ate the bugs?

_____

Harcourt Brace School Publishers

Name _____

Circle the word that names each picture. Then write the word.

SUPER REVIEW

1		2		3	
	limb lamb lame _____		pun pan pen _____		doll dull dill _____

4		5		6	
	trick track truck _____		pine pin pain _____		dune dock double _____

7		8		9	
	bad bud bed _____	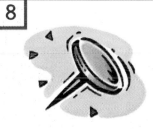	tack tick take _____		hat hot hit _____

10		11		12	
	pot pat pet _____		fine fin fan _____		tub tube tail _____

Harcourt Brace School Publishers

Circle the letter or letters that stand for the short vowel sound in each picture name. Then write the letter or letters that complete the word.

1	i u ou	2	e u a	3	o u e
p____g		c____t		b____lt	

4	a ou e	5	o u e	6	u o e
c____ntry		r____ck		l____g	

7	u e i	8	e a i	9	u o i
r____g		h____m		m____tt	

10	u a e	11	u a i	12	e o a
c____b		p____n		m____p	

Harcourt Brace School Publishers

Fill in the circle next to the word that names the picture.

1
- ○ bat
- ○ bait
- ○ beat

2
- ○ tip
- ○ top
- ○ tap

3
- ○ hall
- ○ hike
- ○ hill

4
- ○ busy
- ○ bus
- ○ best

5
- ○ clock
- ○ cute
- ○ country

6
- ○ check
- ○ chick
- ○ cheek

7
- ○ sack
- ○ sock
- ○ soak

8
- ○ pan
- ○ pine
- ○ pen

9
- ○ rock
- ○ rakc
- ○ road

10
- ○ dark
- ○ duke
- ○ duck

11
- ○ itch
- ○ ox
- ○ ax

12
- ○ kite
- ○ kit
- ○ cot

13
- ○ bag
- ○ big
- ○ bug

14
- ○ tub
- ○ tube
- ○ tab

15
- ○ mat
- ○ mitt
- ○ met

Fill in the circle next to the word that completes each sentence. Then write the word.

1. I like to _____.	○ ruler ○ run ○ rope
2. I can go very _____.	○ fast ○ feast ○ face
3. I have a big _____.	○ dug ○ dog ○ dig
4. He is _____ with white spots.	○ bait ○ blame ○ black
5. My dog likes to run _____ me.	○ wide ○ when ○ with
6. Sometimes he stops to _____.	○ dig ○ dune ○ dime
7. I also have a _____ cat.	○ yet ○ you ○ young

Harcourt Brace School Publishers

Name _____

feather

The word *feather* has the short *e* sound.
Write *ea* to complete each picture name that has
the short *e* sound.

1. tr___sure

2. l___mb

3. c___r

4. br___d

5. f___x

6. sw___ter

7. r___g

8. w___ther

9. v___n

10. br___kfast

11. m___tt

12. thr___d

13. b___s

14. d___ck

15. h___d

Write the word that completes each sentence. You will not use all the words.

feathers	breakfast	bird	meadow	sweater	read
heavy	spread	grass	bread	weather	ready

1. Kate woke up and ate _____.

2. The _____ outside was sunny but cool.

3. Kate wore a _____ to keep her warm.

4. "Are you _____?" Kate asked her friend Nancy.

5. The big picnic basket was _____!

6. The girls walked to a grassy_____.

7. They _____ a blanket on the ground.

8. "Look at the bright _____ on that bird!" said Kate.

9. Kate and Nancy left crumbs of _____ for the bird.

10. After they ate their lunch, the girls _____ a book.

Short Vowel: /e/ea • Reading Words with Short e

Phonics Practice Book

Harcourt Brace School Publishers

The word *rain* has the long *a* sound. If a one-syllable word has two vowels, the first vowel is usually long and the second is usually silent. Write *ai* to complete each picture name that has the long *a* sound.

rain

1	2	3
sn_____l	ch_____n	fl_____g

4	5	6
n_____l	m_____p	tr_____n

7	8	9
b_____d	br_____d	cr_____b

10	11	12
p_____nt	d_____ck	m_____l

13	14	15
c_____t	r_____n	t_____l

The letters *ay* can stand for the long *a* sound. Write *ay* to complete each picture name that has the long *a* sound.

jay

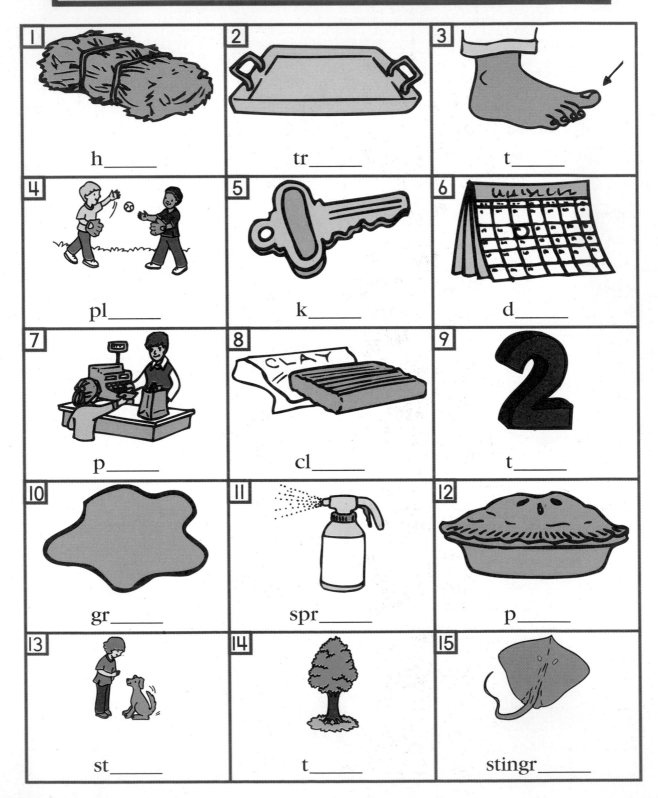

1. h_____

2. tr_____

3. t_____

4. pl_____

5. k_____

6. d_____

7. p_____

8. cl_____

9. t_____

10. gr_____

11. spr_____

12. p_____

13. st_____

14. t_____

15. stingr_____

Harcourt Brace School Publishers

The word *skate* has the long *a* sound. If a one-syllable word has two vowels, the first vowel is usually long and the second is usually silent. Write *a* and *e* to complete each picture name that has the long *a* sound.

sk<u>a</u>t<u>e</u>

1	2	3
wh ___ l	w ___ g	r ___ k
4	5	6
c ___ n	c ___ n	c ___ v
7	8	9
l ___ k	c ___ p	g ___ m
10	11	12
c ___ k	p ___ g	p ___ g
13	14	15
sn ___ k	t ___ p	w ___ v

Name _____

 r<u>ai</u>n   j<u>ay</u>   sk<u>a</u>t<u>e</u>

Circle the word that names each picture. Then write the word.

1  plan / play / plow	**2**  sail / sat / sell	**3**  rack / rock / rake
4 train picture track / trick / train	**5**  wag / wave / win	**6** 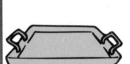 tray / try / trap
7  can / cane / kite	**8**  star / stick / stay	**9**  paint / pants / pints
10  brand / bread / braid	**11**  whale / wall / wade	**12**  raw / ray / rat

Long Vowel *a*

Phonics Practice Book

Harcourt Brace School Publishers

Say the name of each picture. Circle the words in the box that rhyme with it.

1		
	date	bait
	wait	mate
	scat	rat
	gate	sat
	plate	rate

2		
	tale	pail
	fall	trail
	mail	sale
	tall	mat
	sill	ran

3		
	way	may
	man	hill
	say	tray
	day	male
	hat	bay

4		
	try	pain
	rain	lane
	cane	brain
	trap	trim
	stain	man

5		
	make	okay
	take	bake
	back	raid
	wake	fake
	rain	ray

Circle the word that completes the sentence. Then write the word.

1. Jake likes to _____ around the lake.

        scat   sat   skate

2. He wears roller _____, a helmet, and pads.

        scats   skates   scours

3. Pads keep him from getting _____ on his knees and elbows.

        scrapes   scraps   spoils

4. He just seems to _____ past the people walking.

        sail   sack   sill

5. He zooms past the _____ carrier.

        mail   mall   mill

6. As he goes by, he smiles and gives a big _____.

        wave   wig   what

7. Jake skates every _____.

        dale   day   dot

8. Even a hard, cold _____ does not stop him.

        ran   rain   red

9. Someday Jake may win a _____.

        risk   rack   race

10. His friend Ray _____ for him at the end of the trail.

        waits   walls   wish

11. They like to _____ together at a nearby park.

        past   plow   play

12. After they play, the boys like to lie in the _____ of a big tree.

        shack   shade   sad

Name _____

The words in the box are hidden in the puzzle. Some words go down. Some words go across. Find and circle each one.

page	snail	U	T	R	A	Y	C	X	P
skate	clay	X	R	Y	I	W	L	S	A
whale	paint	J	A	Y	T	H	A	K	A
jay	train	I	I	P	L	A	Y	A	I
tray	play	S	N	A	I	L	Z	T	N
		L	P	A	G	E	K	E	T
									R

Write the word from the puzzle that names each picture.

Name _____

Circle the word that fits each clue. Then write the word.

1. It is the long hair on a lion's head. _____

        man   may   mane

2. You can put flowers in it. _____

        vast   vase   vane

3. It is not night. _____

        day   dear   dare

4. You may ride in it on a trip. _____

        train   tray   trap

5. Cows like to eat this. _____

        ha   hay   heat

6. It's where you put your food. _____

        plate   plain   pat

7. It is a place to swim and sail. _____

        lack   lap   lake

8. It is what you do when you talk. _____

        save   say   sat

9. It is a place to keep a picture. _____

        frame   farm   fan

10. It is a way to say hello. _____

        wave   wall   wad

11. It is a blue bird. _____

        jail   lap   jay

Harcourt Brace School Publishers

Circle the sentence that best tells about the picture.

1. Will Dad and Jane bake a cake?

   What can Dad and Jane make?

   Did Jane go out to play?

2. Dad opens the mail.

   Dad gets a tray.

   Dad has some nails.

3. Jane gets out some hay.

   Jane takes out wood scraps.

   Jane plays with a toy train.

4. "This is the way to make it," Dad says.

   "This is the way to play a horn," Dad says.

   "This is a very good cake," Dad says.

5. Jane waves to Dad.

   Jane puts it on a plate.

   Jane paints it.

6. They will place it by the trail.

   They will sail it on the lake.

   They will stay inside all day.

8 eight

veil

The letters *ei* and *eigh* can stand for the long *a* sound. Circle the word that names the picture. Then write the word.

1.
slit
sleigh
sell

_____

2.
reindeer
record
riddle

_____

3.
rests
rings
reins

_____

4.
neighbor
nobody
never

_____

5.
want
weight
wet

_____

6.
egg
art
eight

_____

Write a word from above to complete each sentence.

7. My next-door _____ has an odd pet.

8. It is a _____ with antlers.

9. He has had it for _____ years.

10. It can pull a lot of _____.

11. It can even pull a _____ over the snow.

12. Sometimes I get to hold the _____.

Long Vowel *a* • Reading Words with Long *a*

Phonics Practice Book

Harcourt Brace School Publishers

Name _____

br<u>ea</u>k

The letters *ea* can stand for the long *a* sound. Write the word that answers each clue. You will not use all of the words.

braid	May	page	snail	tray
break	great	paint	steak	wave
hay	neighbor	play	train	whale

1. When you drop a glass, it may do this. _____

2. You can do this on a piano or with a game. _____

3. It is a small, slow animal that lives in a shell. _____

4. This is part of a book. _____

5. It is something you use to make pictures. _____

6. If something is really good, we call it this. _____

7. You can carry food on this. It is larger than a plate. _____

8. This is someone who lives near your home. _____

9. It is something that many people can ride in. It runs on a track.

_____

10. It is a kind of dried grass that a horse likes to eat. _____

11. It is not a fish, but it looks like a big one. It is a huge sea animal.

_____

12. It is something to eat. You can cook it on a grill. _____

Write each word under the correct heading.

baby	crayon	neighbor	plate	snake
baker	lady	weight	reindeer	stingray
clay	mayor	paint	snail	whale

	People	Animals	Things
	_____	_____	_____
	_____	_____	_____
	_____	_____	_____
	_____	_____	_____
	_____	_____	_____

Long Vowel: *a* • Sorting Words with Long *a*

Phonics Practice Book

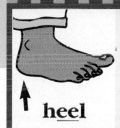

The letters *ee* in *heel* stand for the long *e* sound. If a one-syllable word has two vowels, the first vowel is usually long and the second is usually silent. Write *ee* to complete each picture name that has the long *e* sound.

heel

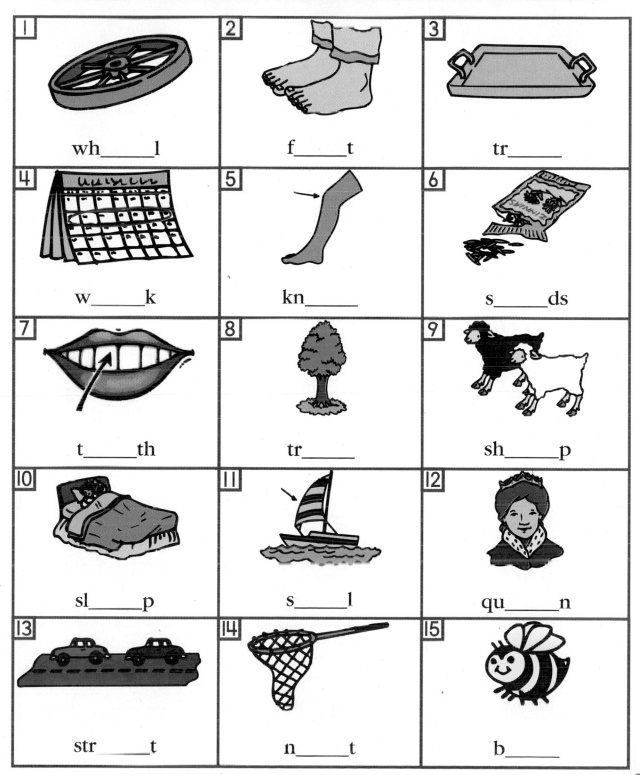

1 wh_____l

2 f_____t

3 tr_____

4 w_____k

5 kn_____

6 s_____ds

7 t_____th

8 tr_____

9 sh_____p

10 sl_____p

11 s_____l

12 qu_____n

13 str_____t

14 n_____t

15 b_____

Name _____

steam

The letters *ea* can stand for the long *ē* sound. If a one-syllable word has two vowels, the first vowel is usually long and the second is usually silent. Write *ea* to complete each picture name that has the long *e* sound.

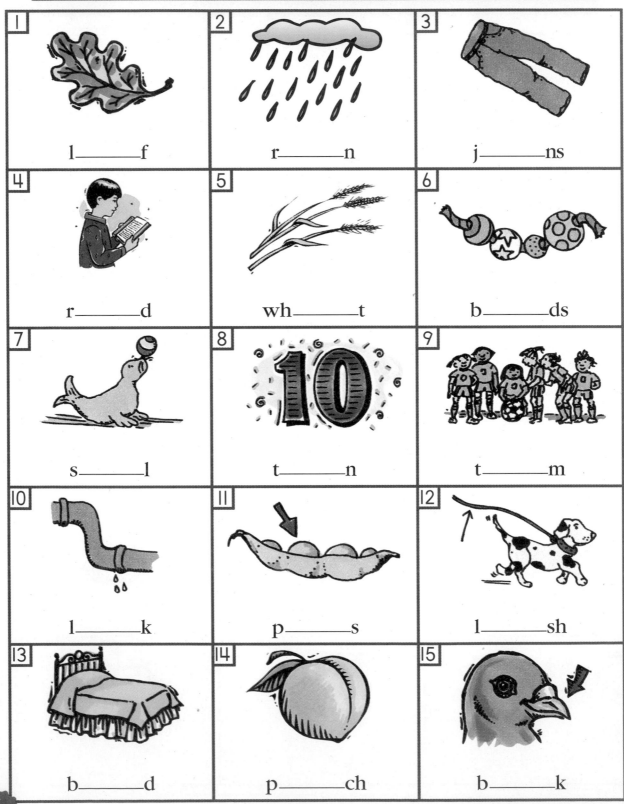

1. l____f
2. r____n
3. j____ns
4. r____d
5. wh____t
6. b____ds
7. s____l
8. t____n
9. t____m
10. l____k
11. p____s
12. l____sh
13. b____d
14. p____ch
15. b____k

Name _____

pupp**y**

When *y* is at the end of a two-syllable word, it usually stands for the long *e* sound. Write *y* to complete each picture name that ends with the long *e* sound.

1 bab___	2 gard___	3 laundr___
4 twent___	5 penn___	6 dadd___
7 jell___	8 cand___	9 cherr___
10 blank___	11 pon___	12 sev___
13 fort___	14 countr___	15 troph___

monkey

When the letters *ey* are at the end of a two-syllable word, they usually stand for the long *e* sound. Write *ey* to complete each picture name that ends with the long *e* sound.

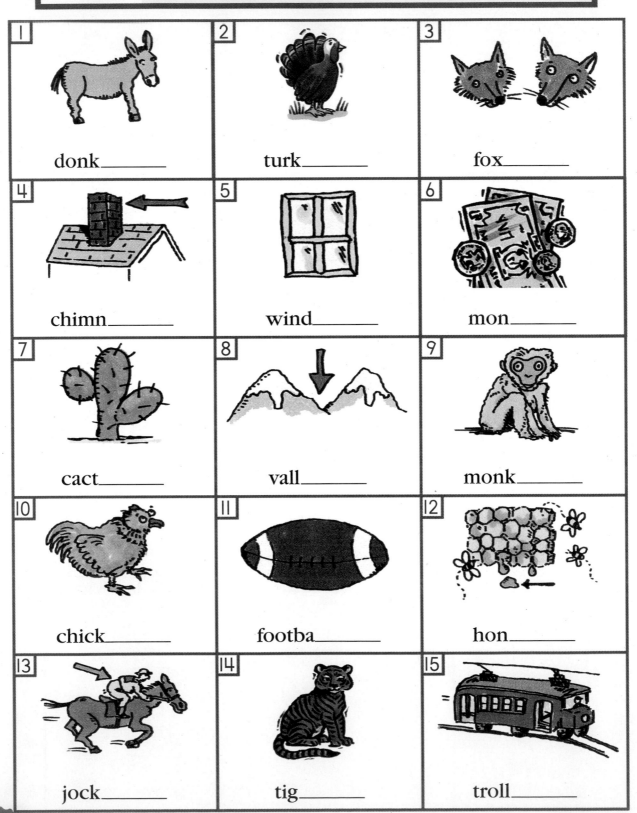

1 donk_____

2 turk_____

3 fox_____

4 chimn_____

5 wind_____

6 mon_____

7 cact_____

8 vall_____

9 monk_____

10 chick_____

11 footba_____

12 hon_____

13 jock_____

14 tig_____

15 troll_____

Phonics Practice Book

Name _____

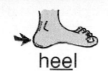 heel   steam   puppy   money

Circle the name of each picture. Then write the word.

1	monkey / money / many	2	cane / keen / queen	3	count / country / cabin
4	jets / jacks / jeans	5	loaf / leaf / left	6	pony / pay / pine
7	many / money / motel	8	tea / try / tree	9	chimney / cheery / candy
10	wake / wreck / week	11	read / rod / red	12	beach / baby / barn
13	laundry / land / lady	14	whale / wheel / will	15	beds / bad / beads

Say the name of each picture. Circle the words that rhyme with it.

1		
	funny	runny
	try	cry
	sunny	bunny
	honey	stay
	tree	clay

2		
	say	dry
	fee	knee
	bee	pea
	tea	see
	Lee	give

3		
	shop	pep
	pay	creep
	deep	beep
	leap	heap
	weep	pie

4		
	holly	golden
	hello	volley
	Polly	folly
	dolly	trail
	pal	jolly

5		
	feel	peel
	deal	real
	mall	mail
	heat	squeal
	meal	wheel

Long Vowel: /ē/ee, ea, ie, y, ey

Phonics Practice Book

Name _____

Circle the word that best completes the sentence. Then write the word.

1. If you get a _____, you must train it and care for it.

    puppy   pipe   padlock

2. You have to _____ it every day.

    feed   foot   fever

3. You also have to give it water _____ day.

    ache   each   enter

4. You need to brush the puppy and protect it from _____.

    flaps   fleas   flutes

5. You _____ to be kind and loving to the puppy.

    next   not   need

6. Training a puppy is never _____.

    eating   easy   eggs

7. You should _____ to it in a soft voice.

    speak   spark   speck

8. You should take it for a walk after each _____.

    men   mail   meal

9. The puppy will have to get used to wearing its _____.

    lash   leak   leash

Name _____

Choose the word that fits each clue. Write the words in the puzzle.

cheek   knee   street
chimney   party   tea
eat   please   teeth
happy   read   turkey
sea

ACROSS

3. A Thanksgiving bird

4. A place where people drive cars

7. Smoke comes out of this

8. What you do at a meal

10. A polite word

11. A large body of water

DOWN

1. A fun gathering of friends

2. What you do with a book

3. What you need to brush often

5. The joint in the middle of your leg

6. The opposite of *sad*

7. A part of your face

9. Something to drink

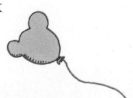

Long Vowel *e* • Reading Words with Long *e*

Phonics Practice Book

Name _____

Circle the word that fits each clue. Then write the word.

1. This is what we do with food. _____

    yet   end   eat

2. This fruit makes a juicy snack. _____

    pest   peach   please

3. The bread we eat is made from this grain. _____

    whale   wheat   wet

4. This small red fruit grows on trees. _____

    cherry   cheer   check

5. Many people grill or bake this food. _____

    met   meat   marry

6. Some people eat this with stuffing and gravy. _____

    turtle   tunnel   turkey

7. Desserts taste this way. _____

    sweet   set   sleep

8. This is a treat you should not eat too often. _____

    city   candy   chimney

9. You should floss these each day. _____

    teach   tell   teeth

10. It is fun to eat meals with them. _____

    feel   family   free

Circle the sentence that tells about the picture.

1. Leesa goes to the beach.
   Leesa loves to read.
   Leesa plants a seed.

2. She enjoys eating.
   She enjoys any kind of story.
   She enjoys seeing the monkey on TV.

3. This book is a good fairy tale.
   This is a big tree.
   This is a good meal.

4. It is about a queen who has a monkey.
   It is about a turkey who loves candy.
   It is about a donkey who turns into a prince.

5. Leesa sees herself in every story.
   Leesa sees the baby in the crib.
   Leesa sees a sheep in the garden.

6. Today she walks her pet dog on a leash.
   Today she is wading in a stream.
   Today she is the girl who made the team.

7. Leesa leaps out of bed every morning.
   Leesa reads every night before she goes to sleep.
   Leesa sleeps with twenty teddy bears.

8. Then she dreams about the story she just read.
   Leesa never has a dream at night.
   Leesa dreams she is weeding the garden.

The letters *ie* can stand for the long *e* sound.
Circle the word that names the picture.

collie

1
keeper
carry
cookie

2
chief
scarf
chest

3
manners
money
movie

4
sheet
shield
shed

5
felt
field
failed

6
brownie
brick
brass

Write the word from the box that best completes each sentence.

thief   believe   shriek   collie   rookie   relief

7. Ernie was a new player—the _____ on the team.

8. Ernie did not _____ he could get a hit.

9. What a _____ it was when he hit the ball!

10. Then Ernie heard a loud _____ .

11. Someone screamed, "Stop, _____!"

12. Ernie's dog, a _____ , had run off with the ball.

Write the word that answers each clue. You will not use all the words.

beak	donkey	knee	seal
bee	easy	neat	sorry
city	honey	peach	teeth

1. It is the name of a pinkish color or a juicy fruit.

   What is it? _____

2. We would not have this sweet treat without bees.

   What is it? _____

3. Does a bird have lips? No, it has this instead.

   What is it? _____

4. It is what you say when you hurt someone's feelings.

   What is it? _____

5. You have these in your mouth and in your comb.

   What are they? _____

6. It sounds like the name of a letter. It is also the name of an insect.

   What is it? _____

7. It is a busy place to live. It is bigger than a town.

   What is it? _____

8. It is the opposite of *messy*.

   What is it? _____

9. It names a sea animal or tells what you do to an envelope.

   What is it? _____

10. Without one of these, your leg would not bend.

    What is it? _____

Harcourt Brace School Publishers

Name _____

Write the word that names the picture.

rein jay tree steak play feet
field snail monkey seal wheel
mail pea cookie train

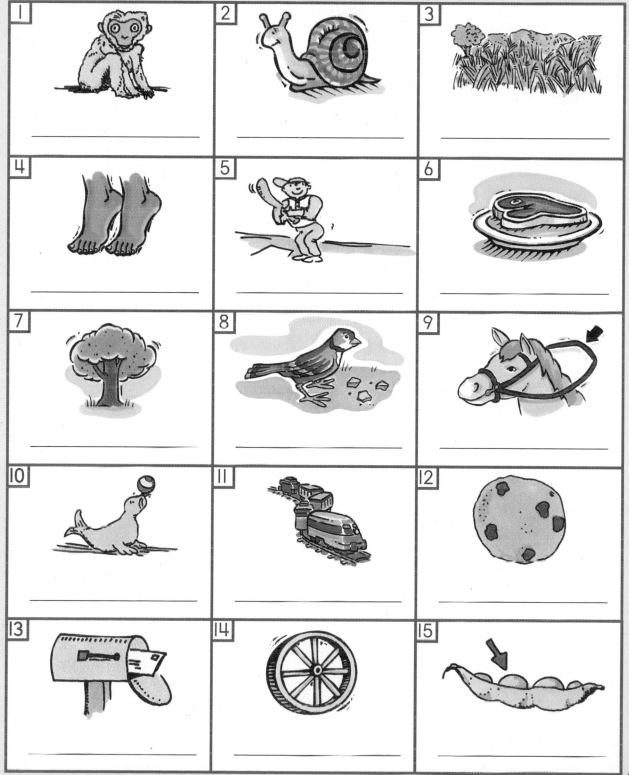

Review of Long Vowels: *a* and *e*

85

Name _____

REVIEW

Read the poem. Then write the answers to the questions.

A Morning Sail

Lee goes out in his sailboat
At the very break of day.
Lee lives right down beside the beach.
He starts each day this way.

Lee waves to all the neighbors
He sees along the way—
To fishers with their pails of bait
And farmers raking hay.

The journey is a brief one.
He pulls into the bay.
But Lee is always happy
When he starts his day this way.

1. Where does Lee live?

_____

2. What does Lee go out in?

_____

3. Who does Lee see each day?

_____

Harcourt Brace School Publishers

If a one-syllable word has two vowels, the first vowel is usually long and the second is usually silent. Write *i* and *e* to complete each picture name that has the long *i* sound.

k**ite**

1
m___c___

2
sl___d___

3
n___n___

4
f___sh

5
b___t___

6
h___v___

7
p___p___

8
sm___l___

9
l___f___

10
d___m___

11
p___n___

12
b___k___

13
c___k___

14
d___v___

15
str___k___

tie

The letters *ie* can stand for the long *i* sound.
Write *ie* to complete each picture name that has the
long *i* sound.

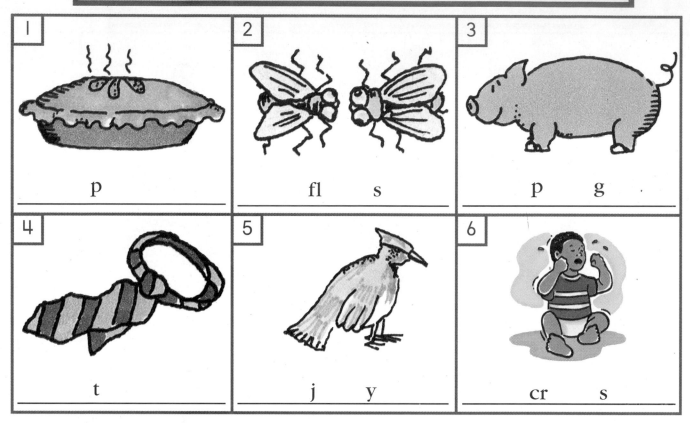

1. p _____

2. fl _____ s

3. p _____ g

4. t _____

5. j _____ y

6. cr _____ s

Write the word that best completes each sentence.

dries   fries   lies   tries

7. The dog _____ by the fire.

8. Cindy _____ to win the race.

9. Sam _____ the dishes.

10. Lauren likes to eat french _____.

Harcourt Brace School Publishers

The letters *igh* stand for the long *i* sound. Fill in the letters *igh* when the picture name has the long *i* sound.

light

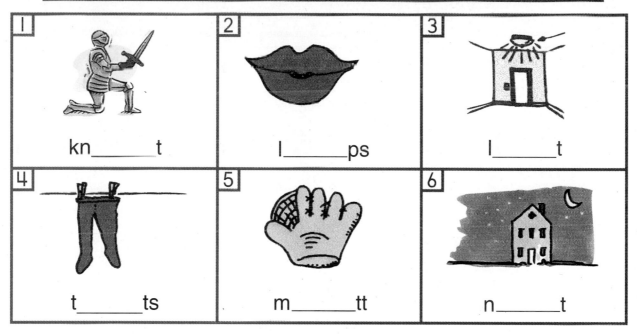

1	2	3
kn____t	l____ps	l____t

4	5	6
t____ts	m____tt	n____t

Write the word that best completes each sentence. You will not use all the words.

    right   bite   bright   fright   flight   bridge

7	The driver turned on her _____ lights to see the road better.
8	Juan takes a late-night _____ to visit his grandmother.
9	The officer tells Jay to turn _____ at the next traffic light.

When *y* is at the end of a one-syllable word, it usually stands for the long *i* sound. Write *y* to complete each picture name that ends with the long *i* sound.

dr<u>y</u>

1. fl____

2. s____

3. sk____

4. cr____

5. tr____

6. dr____

7. pl____

8. tr____

9. j____

10. fr____

11. s____

12. sh____

Harcourt Brace School Publishers

kite   tie   light   dry

Circle the word that names each picture. Then write the word.

1	pea pie pay	2	slid sleep slide	3	stay skip sky
_____		_____		_____	

4	high hip hay	5	miss mice mike	6	dim dream dime
_____		_____		_____	

7	tea tame tie	8	knight knee knit	9	flees flies fleas
_____		_____		_____	

10	pine pin pain	11	strips straps stripes	12	dress dries dream
_____		_____		_____	

13	frees fries frays	14	bite bit bait	15	fray free fry
_____		_____		_____	

Name _____

Hide and Go Seek

It's hide-and-go-seek time.
Let's get out of sight.
This time they won't find us
If they hunt all night!

I'll lie on the branch of
This nice old tree,
And you hide behind it
As still as can be.

I wish we could fly high
Up in the sky.
Where they couldn't find us
They'd never guess why!

Write the answers to the questions.

1. What game does the poem tell about?

_____

2. What does the speaker have to do?

_____

3. Where does the speaker hide?

_____

4. Where does the speaker wish they could hide?

_____

Write the word that best completes the sentence.

midnight	quite	beside	try	tried	my	fright
smile	light	dine	right	time	outside	flashlight

1. The clock struck _____.

2. Mike heard a crash _____ the house.

3. Mike _____ to hide under the covers.

4. He shook with _____.

5. Then Dad turned on the _____.

6. "Are you all _____?" asked Dad.

7. "Do you know what is _____?" Mike asked.

8. Dad had a _____ in his hand.

9. Mike was not _____ sure that they should go see.

10. He decided to _____ to be brave.

11. "Oh _____!" laughed Mike.

12. He gave a _____ of delight.

13. Two raccoons had come to _____.

14. They were having a great _____!

Harcourt Brace School Publishers

The words below are in the puzzle. Some words go down, and some words go across. Find and circle each one.

| bike | cries | flies | knight | light |
| pie | pine | sky | side | smile |

```
X P I N E S K Y
L I G H T Y R X
Y E F L I E S B
K N I G H T X I
S M I L E Z Y K
C R I E S I D E
```

Write the word from the puzzle that names each picture.

1	2
3	4
5	6
7	8

Write the word that fits each clue. You will not use all of the words.

why	bike	mile	light	fright	slide
bright	sight	lie	size	tie	fly	pic	file

1. It is something to ride that has only two wheels.

   _____

2. It means "not heavy" or "not dark." _____

3. It is fun to bake and good to eat. _____

4. It is a scared feeling. _____

5. This is a long way to walk. _____

6. This word often begins a question. _____

7. You can wear one of these or do it to your shoelaces.

   _____

8. It is one of your five senses. _____

9. George Washington said he could not tell one. _____

10. It is something both a bird and an airplane can do. _____

11. It can be small, medium, or large. _____

12. It is something you might see in a park or what you do into

    home plate. _____

Harcourt Brace School Publishers

Circle the sentence that tells about the picture.

1	"Here is a kite," said Mama Bird. "Go to sleep. It is night," said Mama Bird. "It is time to fly," said Mama Bird.
2	Baby Bird had a bite to eat. Baby Bird looked up at the sky. Baby Bird went down the slide.
3	"I will need a flashlight up there," she said. "I will ride a bike up there," she said. "I will have a fine time up there," she said.
4	Then Baby Bird looked down from the pine. Then Baby Bird fried leaves in a pan. Then Baby Bird went on a hayride.
5	Baby Bird slid down the vine. Baby Bird was filled with fright. Baby Bird cheeped with delight.
6	"No!" cried Baby Bird. "It is too high." "Yes!" cried Baby Bird. "I would love some pie." "Oh, dear!" cried Baby Bird. "I need a new tie."
7	Rain began falling from the sky. Baby Bird could not fly. Baby Bird could fly!
8	Now Baby Bird rides on the train. Now Baby Bird flies all the time. Now Baby Bird sits in the pine.

When the letter **i** is followed by **nd, ld,** or **gn,** it often stands for the long **i** sound.

behi<u>nd</u>   **chi<u>ld</u>**   **si<u>gn</u>**

Write the word that answers each question.

behind   bind   child   find   kind
mind   blinds   rind   sign   wild   wind

1. Which word is the opposite of *lose*? _____

2. Which word names what you use to think? _____

3. Which word tells what you do when you write your name? _____

4. Which word is the opposite of *tame*? _____

5. Which word means "to tie with string"? _____

6. Which word names something that covers a window? _____

7. Which word is the opposite of *in front of*? _____

8. Which word can name the skin of a fruit? _____

9. Which word tells what you do to keep some clocks running? _____

10. Which word is the opposite of *mean*? _____

11. Which word names a person who is still very young? _____

Look at the picture. Then follow the directions.

1. Draw window blinds on one window.

2. On the other window write *Pop's Diner.*

3. Write *Try it!* at the bottom of the sign.

4. Circle the frying pans on the wall.

5. Mark an X on the diner's tie.

6. Draw a glass of milk beside the slice of pie.

7. Draw a table knife in the boy's hand.

8. Add a napkin beside the child's plate.

Now circle all the long *i* words in the directions.

Name _____

The word *soap* has the long *o* sound. If a one-syllable word has two vowels, the first vowel is usually long and the second is usually silent. Write *oa* to complete each picture name that has the long *o* sound.

soap

1 c____t

2 d____g

3 b____t

4 c____t

5 l____f

6 r____d

7 c____l

8 s____l

9 g____t

10 fl____t

11 f____t

12 t____st

13 t____d

14 h____t

15 c____ch

Harcourt Brace School Publishers

Name _____

r<u>o</u>se

The word *rose* has the long *o* sound.
Write *o* and *e* to complete each picture name that
has the long *o* sound.

1	2	3
c _ n	n _ s	n _ t

4	5	6
r _ p	p _ t	ph _ n

7	8	9
h _ s	sm _ k	sl _ d

10	11	12
r _ b	st _ v	b _ n

13	14	15
sn _ k	t _ p	gl _ b

The letters *ow* can stand for the long *o* sound.
Write *ow* to complete each picture name that has
the long *o* sound.

crow

1. thr _____	2. sn _____	3. tr _____
4. pill _____	5. arr _____	6. monk _____
7. p _____	8. rainb _____	9. b _____ l
10. h _____	11. cr _____	12. m _____
13. wind _____	14. bl _____	15. shad _____

Name_____

 soap  rose   crow

Circle the word that names each picture. Then write the word.

1	coat / cot / crate	2	nose / nod / nice	3	bait / box / boat
4	phone / pond / pain	5	raining / ribbon / rainbow	6	snail / snow / sob
7	arrow / arm / armor	8	rope / rod / ripe	9	glad / glob / globe
10	rate / road / rod	11	cost / cash / coach	12	tied / toad / top
13	tow / tea / ton	14	night / not / note	15	shopping / shadow / shading

Harcourt Brace School Publishers

Name _____

Load up the big semi,
Then start up and go.
This rig can't be stopped
By rain or by snow.

One goal has the driver,
Who lives on the road—
Get the goods there on time,
Then quickly unload.

Pick up a new load
In the loading zone,
Then back on the road again—
Always alone.

1. What must the driver of a big rig do before setting out?

   _____

2. What cannot stop this driver's rig?

   _____

3. What is every truck driver's goal?

   _____

4. Where does the driver pick up a new load?

   _____

5. What would be a good title for the poem?

   _____

Now underline the long *o* words in the poem.

Circle the word that best completes the sentence. Then write the word.

1. The _____ ate Farmer Rose's corn.
   cots   crates   crows

2. Farmer Rose went _____ very angry.
   home   him   honey

3. "I will _____ them," he said.
   sob   show   say

4. "I will make a _____ ."
   scarecrow   saddle   soccer

5. At home, Mrs. Rose was on the _____ .
   fog   phone   fun

6. She did not _____ what Farmer Rose was up to.
   cob   cake   know

7. Farmer Rose got Mrs. Rose's _____ .
   rob   read   robe

8. He got a _____ for a hat.
   bill   bowl   bond

9. He needed a _____ to finish the scarecrow.
   pole   pond   par

10. That night Mrs. Rose looked high and _____ for her robe.
    lie   low   lot

11. Then she looked out the _____ .
    window   wife   wall

12. "Oh, no," _____ Mrs. Rose.
    grain   got   groaned

13. "You should have _____ I would need my robe."
    kind   known   kid

14. "Well," said Farmer Rose, "may I use your _____ instead?"
    kite   cat   coat

Name _____

Write the word in the puzzle that fits each clue.

coach   coal   doze   drove   hole   home   phone
pillow   rainbow   road   shadow   soap   window

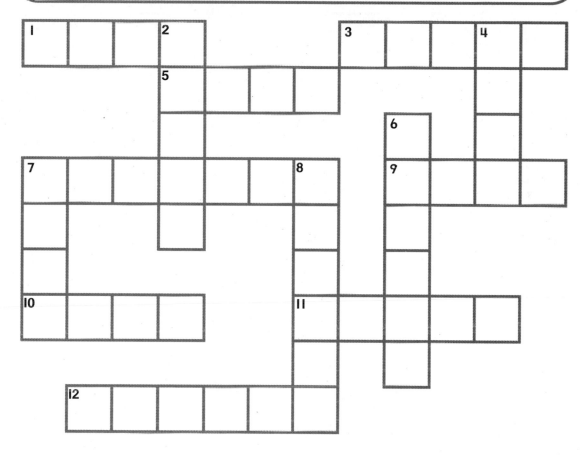

Across
1. You wash your hands with it.
3. The teacher of a sports team
5. People live here.
7. Bright colors in the sky
9. Something you can dig
10. To take a short nap
11. What Mom did with the car
12. A soft place for your head

Down
2. What you use to call people
4. People get it from a mine.
6. It follows you on a sunny day.
7. A place to drive a car
8. Something to look out of

Write the word that fits each clue.

foal	rope	hole	slow	globe
low	mow	phone	oats	throne
float	woke	croak	roast	joke

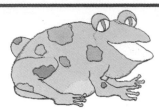

1. You tell one to make people laugh. _____

2. You can tie things up with this. _____

3. When it rings, you pick it up. _____

4. It is the sound a frog makes. _____

5. You do this to food in your oven. _____

6. This is something you can do in the water. _____

7. A horse thinks this is a treat. _____

8. It is a map in the shape of the Earth. _____

9. This is something you make when you dig. _____

10. It is the opposite of *high*. _____

11. It is a chair for a king or a queen. _____

12. It is the first thing you did this morning. _____

13. It is something you do to grass. _____

14. It is the opposite of *fast*. _____

15. It is a name for a baby horse. _____

Harcourt Brace School Publishers

Circle the sentence that tells about the picture.

1. Joan and Mom load up the car.
   Joan and Mom get on their bikes.
   Joan and Mom are on the phone.

2. They see a rainbow in the snow.
   They float on their backs down the stream.
   They go to the cove by the lake.

3. They like to stay home.
   They eat ice-cream cones.
   They get into the boat.

4. They phone home from the park.
   They row to the park.
   They run up the slope.

5. Mom ties the boat with a rope.
   Mom floats away in the boat.
   Joan likes to jump rope.

6. It looks as if they are all alone.
   They put on their coats.
   They look at the globe.

7. Mom broke the rope.
   Mom cooks oats on the stove.
   Soon smoke will rise from the fire.

8. They dig a hole.
   They roast hot dogs.
   They pick a rose.

Name _____

 zero The letter *o* can stand for the long *o* sound.
Write the word that names the picture.

yolk   roll   cold   zero   gold   comb

1. _____

2. _____

3. _____

4. _____

5. _____

6. _____

Write the word that best completes each sentence.

over   colt   fold   go   hold   old

7. This _____ game is still fun to play.

8. Draw a _____ without a tail.

9. Then _____ a big scarf to make
a blindfold.

10. Tie the blindfold _____ your eyes.

11. In your hand, _____ the colt's tail.

12. Now _____ to the colt, and try
to pin the tail to the right spot.

Long Vowel *o* • Reading Words with Long *o*   Phonics Practice Book

Harcourt Brace School Publishers

Write the word that answers each clue.

bowl	elbow	note	rose
coat	grow	rainbow	show
code	hose	rope	slow

1. You can water a garden with it. _____

2. You can jump with it or tie something with it. _____

3. It is the name of a flower. _____

4. It means "not fast." _____

5. You wear one when it is cold outside. _____

6. If the sun shines through rain, you may see one of these.

_____

7. It is a short letter or a part of a song. _____

8. Your address has a ZIP _____.

9. It is another name for a movie. _____

10. It is something you eat cereal and other foods out of.

_____

11. A plant does it quickly. You do it too, but slowly. _____

12. You can bend your arm because you have this.

Read the paragraphs and answer the questions.

SECRET CODES

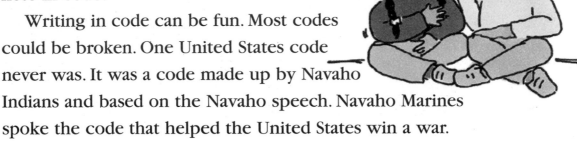

Would you like to write a note to a friend that no one else can read? Then write your note in code!

Writing in code can be fun. Most codes could be broken. One United States code never was. It was a code made up by Navaho Indians and based on the Navaho speech. Navaho Marines spoke the code that helped the United States win a war.

There are many ways to make up your own codes. You can write your note backward, like this: .eert kao eht ta em teeM

You can also make up a number code. For an easy number code, use 1 for *A*, 2 for *B*, and so on. This code is shown below:

1=A	2=B	3=C	4=D	5=E	6=F	7=G	8=H
9=I	10=J	11=K	12=L	13=M	14=N	15=O
16=P	17=Q	18=R	19=S	20=T	21=U	22=V
23=W	24=X	25=Y	26=Z

1. Who made up a code that was never broken? _____

2. Decode this message:

    14 15 23 / 25 15 21 / 11 14 15 23 / 1 12 12 /

    1 2 15 21 20 / 12 15 14 7 / 15.

    _____

    _____

Name _____

Circle the letter or letters that stand for the long vowel sound in the picture name. Then write the word.

REVIEW

1	i-e ai oa _____

2	ay ie oa _____

3	i-e a-e o-e _____

4	i-e ow ea _____

5	igh o-e ea _____

6	ea ai oa _____

7	a-e igh oa	night _____

8	ow ie a-e _____

9	y ea o-e _____

10	ie ow ea _____

11	ee ai ie _____

12	oa a-e igh _____

13	o i-e ai _____

14	ee i-e ai _____

15	ie ay ea _____

REVIEW Read the poem. Then write the answers to the questions.

Showtime at the Fair

Di will show her new colt.
Joan will show her pet goat.
Joe's fine golden duckling
Will dive and float.

Bo has baby chicks
That cannot fly high.
They hide behind Mother Hen
Tiny and shy.

I ride a white pony
Just right for my size.
Oh, here come the judges—
Hope I win a prize!

Harcourt Brace School Publishers

1. What will Di and Joan show?

_____

2. What do the baby chicks do?

_____

3. What will the judges do?

_____

4. What pet will the speaker of the poem show?

_____

The word *mule* has the long *u* sound.
Write the letters *u* and *e* to complete each picture
name that has the long *u* sound.

mule

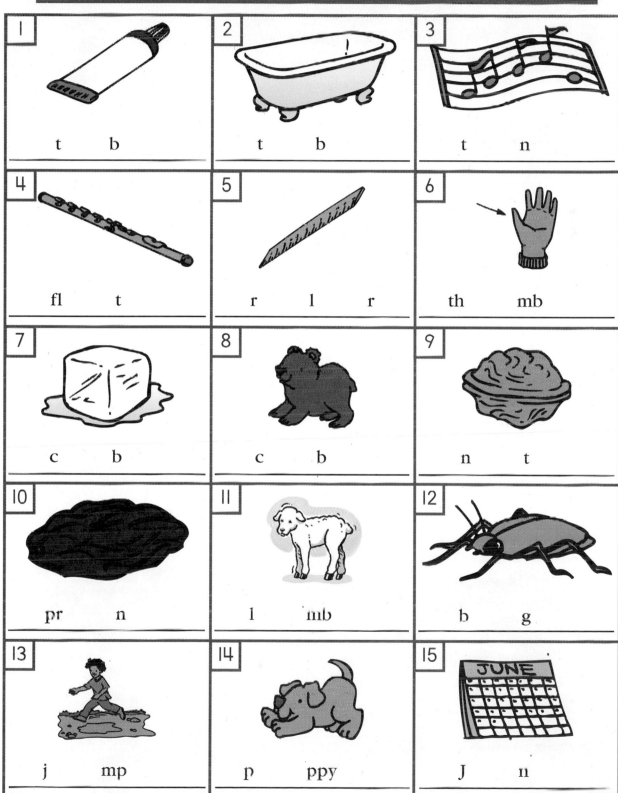

1	2	3
t____b	t____b	t____n

4	5	6
fl____t	r____l____r	th____mb

7	8	9
c____b	c____b	n____t

10	11	12
pr____n	l____mb	b____g

13	14	15
j____mp	p____ppy	J____n

Long Vowel: /yo͞o/*u-e*

Read the poem. Then write the answers to the questions.

Come march to our tune.
Bring your flute to play.
We're going to have
A parade today.

We'll wear uniforms
And hats with plumes,
While some twirl batons
In cute costumes.

1. What are the children going to do?

   _____

2. What does the speaker invite a friend to do?

   _____

3. What would be a good title for the poem?

   _____

Long Vowel: /yōō/*u-e* • Reading Words in Context

Phonics Practice Book

Circle the word that best completes the sentence. Then write the word.

1. Try not to be _____ .

    red   rude   run

2. Push toothpaste from the bottom of the _____ .

    tab   tub   tube

3. Don't _____ to share.

    recall   reef   refuse

4. Don't _____ the Earth with litter.

    pollute   pillow   polo

5. Be kind to animals, even _____ .

    miles   mules   mugs

6. Say thank you if someone says you're _____ .

    curl   cute   cutter

7. Try to follow the _____ when you sing.

    tune   ton   tulip

8. Chewing ice _____ may break a tooth.

    canes   cubes   cubs

9. Throw your dirty clothes in the laundry _____ .

    shut   chain   chute

10. Keep the _____ down on your radio.

    valley   volume   very

11. Don't _____ your brother's toys.

    use   as   us

12. Don't make too many _____ .

    rules   rolls   rails

The words below are in the puzzle. Some words go down. Some words go across. Find and circle each one.

chute   cube   dune   flute   June   mule
plume   pollute   tube   tune   cute

X	A	R	F	T	H	I	C
P	O	L	L	U	T	E	H
L	I	C	U	B	E	J	U
U	C	U	T	E	Z	U	T
M	U	L	E	T	U	N	E
E	Z	D	U	N	E	E	U

Write the word from the puzzle that names each picture. You will not use all of the words.

1. _____

2. _____

3. _____

4. _____

5. _____

6. _____

Long Vowel: /yōō/u-e

Phonics Practice Book

Write the word that fits each clue.

tune	cube	parachute	June	mule	flute
plume	huge	costume	cute	spruce	pollute

1. It is an animal that is like a horse. _____

2. It is the opposite of tiny. _____

3. People play pretty music on this. _____

4. It is a month of the year. _____

5. It is the feather on a hat. _____

6. It's what people say babies are. _____

7. Our planet will stay clean if we don't do this. _____

8. You can play or sing this. _____

9. You may wear this if you act in a play. _____

10. It is a kind of tree. _____

11. You'd better wear this if you jump out of a plane. _____

12. It is a word for a square piece of ice. _____

Circle the sentence that tells about the picture.

1.

In June, Luke went to a dude ranch.

In June, Luke had flute lessons.

In June, Luke slid down a dune.

2.

Luke wore a mule costume.

Luke wore a grand duke costume.

Luke wore a cowhand outfit.

3.

His job was to cut down a huge spruce.

His job was to feed the mules.

His job was to write the rules.

4.

Luke used a flute for the first time.

Luke rode a huge horse for the first time.

Luke pruned a tree for the first time.

5.

He petted a huge mule.

He petted a bird with a plumed tail.

He petted a cute baby calf.

6.

The cowhands sang and played tunes.

The cowhands were rude.

The cowhands refused to smile.

Harcourt Brace School Publishers

Circle the word that names each picture. Then write the word.

1.
try
tree
tray

_____

2.
mule
mile
meal

_____

3.
whale
while
wheel

_____

4.
sneak
snake
snow

_____

5.
late
light
lute

_____

6.
goat
gate
greet

_____

7.
tea
tie
tow

_____

8.
mule
need
nail

_____

9.
came
climb
comb

_____

10.
sole
sail
seal

_____

11.
true
tray
tree

_____

12.
reap
ripe
rope

_____

13.
bike
bake
beak

_____

14.
flows
flees
flies

_____

15.
crow
cry
creep

_____

Circle the sentence that tells about the picture.

1. The whale slides down the chute.

   Whales like to ride in boats.

   A whale is a huge animal.

2. Look at the frisky colts.

   Goats and mules graze at the farm.

   Goats and mules sleep in the house.

3. White mice make good pets.

   The mice are eating ice cream.

   The white mice are running away.

4. Most people do not like flies.

   The plane is high up in the sky.

   Some people do not like to cry.

5. A wild bunny does not have a tail.

   A wild bunny likes to fly.

   A wild bunny is often shy.

6. The seal is on the beach.

   Seals can do funny tricks.

   The seal is in the seat.

7. Bats like to fly at night.

   Bats fly when it is light.

   A bat cannot fly.

8. The snail is in the pail.

   Cats have sharp nails.

   Snails are very slow.

Harcourt Brace School Publishers

Name _____

1
- ○ crack
- ○ cry
- ○ crow

2
- ○ scat
- ○ skate
- ○ skirt

3
- ○ seal
- ○ sell
- ○ sale

4
- ○ meal
- ○ mill
- ○ mule

5
- ○ cot
- ○ coat
- ○ cute

6
- ○ monkey
- ○ milky
- ○ muddy

7
- ○ bin
- ○ bone
- ○ burn

8
- ○ pint
- ○ pant
- ○ paint

9
- ○ field
- ○ fold
- ○ fade

10
- ○ pay
- ○ pea
- ○ pie

11
- ○ flat
- ○ flute
- ○ float

12
- ○ hay
- ○ ha
- ○ hi

13
- ○ cope
- ○ cap
- ○ cape

14
- ○ knight
- ○ knee
- ○ knit

15
- ○ pen
- ○ pillow
- ○ penny

Fill in the circle next to the letters that stand for the long vowel sound in each picture name. Then write the word.

1	○ ow ○ ie ○ ea	2	○ ee ○ igh ○ ay	3	○ u-e ○ ai ○ ie

4	○ i-e ○ ay ○ ea	5	○ u-e ○ a-e ○ ea	6	○ igh ○ ow ○ ea

7	○ ow ○ u-e ○ ey	8	○ u-e ○ a-e ○ o-e	9	○ ow ○ ay ○ ea

10	○ ea ○ oa ○ igh	11	○ a-e ○ ow ○ igh	12	○ ea ○ u-e ○ ow

13	○ i-e ○ a-e ○ o-e	14	○ ow ○ ay ○ igh	15	○ ow ○ ee ○ igh

Harcourt Brace School Publishers

Read each word. If the word has a long vowel sound, circle *long*. If the word has a short vowel sound, circle *short*.

REVIEW

1	hot	long	short
2	ring	long	short
3	game	long	short
4	belt	long	short
5	life	long	short
6	swim	long	short
7	sweet	long	short
8	camp	long	short
9	tent	long	short
10	flute	long	short
11	bowl	long	short
12	sight	long	short
13	trunk	long	short
14	sock	long	short
15	tune	long	short
16	pig	long	short
17	coal	long	short
18	young	long	short
19	treat	long	short
20	fry	long	short

REVIEW Circle the name of each picture. Then write the word.

1. mart
   mat
   mitt
   _____

2. kite
   kit
   kick
   _____

3. fan
   fort
   feet
   _____

4. note
   net
   not
   _____

5. bead
   bed
   bad
   _____

6. it
   eat
   eight
   _____

7. tab
   tub
   tube
   _____

8. ran
   rule
   rain
   _____

9. rod
   red
   road
   _____

10. man
    main
    mean
    _____

11. cat
    coat
    cot
    _____

12. sell
    sale
    seal
    _____

13. mule
    mole
    mail
    _____

14. cane
    kind
    can
    _____

15. neat
    net
    night
    _____

Harcourt Brace School Publishers

Review of Short and Long Vowels   Phonics Practice Book

Name _____

Circle the word that best completes the sentence. Then write the word.

REVIEW

1. There are many ways to _____ between two places.

      rid   ride   road

2. You can go by rail on a _____.

      train   tan   try

3. You can _____ down a slope on your bike.

      cost   cat   coast

4. You can row a boat down a _____.

      stream   stem   strap

5. You can _____ in a plane.

      fill   flea   fly

6. You _____ like to take a bus.

      might   met   mitt

7. In the winter, ride in a _____ down a snowy path.

      slap   slid   sleigh

8. A jockey rides a _____ racing horse.

      face   fast   fist

9. Children might roller _____ down the sidewalk.

      scat   skate   skit

10. You might even ride a _____ on a dusty trail.

      mule   mug   mile

11. Of course, that would be a slow _____ .

      try   trip   tray

Fill in the circle next to the word that names each picture.

1.
- ○ vain
- ○ van
- ○ phone

2.
- ○ tab
- ○ tub
- ○ tube

3.
- ○ tent
- ○ tint
- ○ tone

4.
- ○ club
- ○ call
- ○ colt

5.
- ○ field
- ○ fell
- ○ failed

6.
- ○ ham
- ○ hum
- ○ home

7.
- ○ shop
- ○ ship
- ○ shape

8.
- ○ skate
- ○ skip
- ○ sky

9.
- ○ rag
- ○ rug
- ○ rage

10.
- ○ night
- ○ not
- ○ neat

11.
- ○ plow
- ○ play
- ○ plead

12.
- ○ big
- ○ bake
- ○ bag

13.
- ○ sock
- ○ soak
- ○ sick

14.
- ○ city
- ○ sight
- ○ kite

15.
- ○ cube
- ○ cob
- ○ cub

Short and Long Vowels Test

Phonics Practice Book

Harcourt Brace School Publishers

Name _____

CHECK-UP

1
- ○ i
- ○ ai
- ○ i-e

_____

2
- ○ ay
- ○ igh
- ○ ee

_____

3
- ○ a
- ○ ie
- ○ u

_____

4
- ○ ow
- ○ a-e
- ○ o-e

_____

5
- ○ u-e
- ○ i
- ○ e

_____

6
- ○ a-e
- ○ i-e
- ○ ee

_____

7
- ○ o
- ○ ow
- ○ ay

_____

8
- ○ e
- ○ i
- ○ o-e

_____

9
- ○ y
- ○ u
- ○ ea

_____

10
- ○ ai
- ○ y
- ○ ow

_____

11
- ○ oa
- ○ ai
- ○ cy

_____

12
- ○ u
- ○ ee
- ○ u-e

_____

13
- ○ ay
- ○ ie
- ○ o

_____

14
- ○ igh
- ○ o
- ○ ea

_____

15
- ○ u-e
- ○ a
- ○ ow

_____

Harcourt Brace School Publishers

Find the name of each picture. Write the word on the line.

star

shark   jar   harp   dart   artist   car   cart
barn   yarn   yard   arm   garden

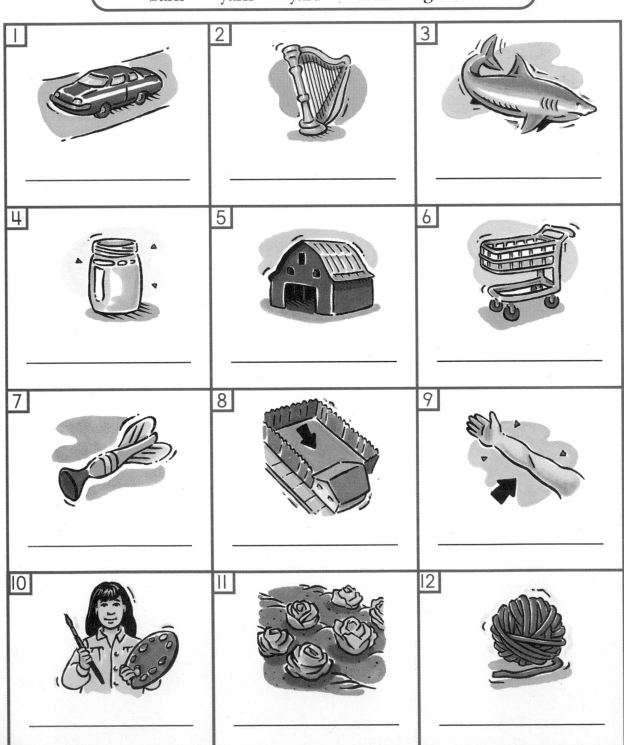

R-controlled Vowel: /är/ *ar*

Phonics Practice Book

Harcourt Brace School Publishers

Name _____

Choose the word that answers each riddle. Write the word on the line. You will not use all the words.

> smart   shark   car   barn   score
> park   chair   scarf   bean

1. I have sharp teeth and swim in the sea. I am a _____.

2. I am a home for farm animals. I am a _____.

3. When you get in, I can take you far. I am a _____.

4. You can play on my swings. I am bigger than your yard.

    I am a _____.

5. You wear me to keep warm. I am a _____.

> jar   farm   harp   card   cart
> bark   hair   jam   bank   star

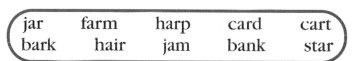

6. Look for me in the sky when it's dark. I am a _____.

7. Many people say my music sounds pretty. I am a _____.

8. My lid can be hard to open. I am a _____.

9. I cover a tree trunk. I am _____.

10. Shoppers put things in me. I am a _____.

11. You get me in the mail on your birthday. I am a _____.

12. Work starts here when the animals wake up.

    I am a _____.

Name _____

Find the name of each picture. Write the word on the line.

turkey

fern

hammer   tiger   spur   curl   letter   baker   turtle
purse   clerk   shower   battery   turkey

1. _____
2. _____
3. _____
4. _____
5. _____
6. _____
7. _____
8. _____
9. _____
10. _____
11. _____
12. _____

R-controlled Vowel: /ûr/*er, ur*

Phonics Practice Book

Write the word that completes the sentence.

curl   fur   turtle   sister   water

1. My _____ just got a new pet.

2. It's a big, brown _____ .

3. She gives it plenty of _____ .

4. My pet cat has soft, warm _____ .

5. I like to watch my cat _____ his tail.

person   turn   letter   her   term

6. I got a _____ in the mail.

7. It was from a _____ I know.

8. She moved away last school _____ .

9. I went to see _____ new house.

10. Now it is her _____ to stay with me!

bird

Write the word that names each picture.

stir	dirt	thirty	girl	bird	shirt	third	skirt

1. _____

2. _____

3. _____

4. _____

5. _____

6. _____

7. _____

8. _____

Write the word that answers each clue. You will not use all the words.

dirt	third	stir	dart	shirt	spur

9. You might wear this with shorts. _____

10. If you are number three, you are this. _____

11. You might dig in this to make a garden. _____

12. You do this to mix a cake. _____

R-controlled Vowel: /ûr/ *ir*

Phonics Practice Book

Harcourt Brace School Publishers

Look at the picture. Then do what the sentences tell you.

1. Add stripes to the woman's shirt.

2. Draw an X above the young girl.

3. Draw a box around the person who is third in line.

4. Show the sound the bird makes. Write *chirp* twice by the bird.

5. Circle the man's shirt.

6. Finish the girl's sentence. She calls the man *sir*.

7. Finish the price tag on the bird's cage. The bird costs thirty dollars.

Name _____

1

We gave Mother a pearl necklace.

We gave Mother a pretty ring.

We earned the money to get a pet.

2

The TV show came on early.

We heard the news on the radio.

We heard the news on TV.

3

We heard a funny story.

We leave on buses after school.

We learn at school.

4

I earn money by selling newspapers.

I like to ride my bike.

I learned how to play ball in gym class.

5

I heard a thunderstorm.

I get up early every morning.

I eat breakfast every morning.

6

We live in a house.

We earn money.

We are learning about planet Earth.

Read the story. Then answer the questions.

Jack's Fishing Trip

One day Jack went to visit his aunt and uncle. His uncle Earl and his aunt Pearl were very happy to see him.

Jack said he wanted to learn to fish. Earl promised to take him early the next morning. So Pearl packed some lunch for Jack and Earl and wished them good luck.

Jack was very excited as he heard the motor on the boat start with a loud *varoom.* That morning Jack caught three fish. Earl said Jack learned very quickly.

When they got home that night, Earl and Jack cleaned the fish. Jack helped Pearl cook them. Earl gave Jack his very own fishing pole. Earl told Jack that he had earned it! Jack cannot wait until his next visit!

1. Why do you think Aunt Pearl and Uncle Earl were glad to see Jack?

_____

2. For how long did Jack and his uncle fish?

_____

3. What did Jack learn to do very quickly?

_____

4. How did Jack earn his own fishing pole?

_____

Harcourt Brace School Publishers

Name _____

Choose the word that fits each clue. Write the word in the puzzle.

car   jar   fur   bird   earth   shark
skirt   fern   curl   pearl

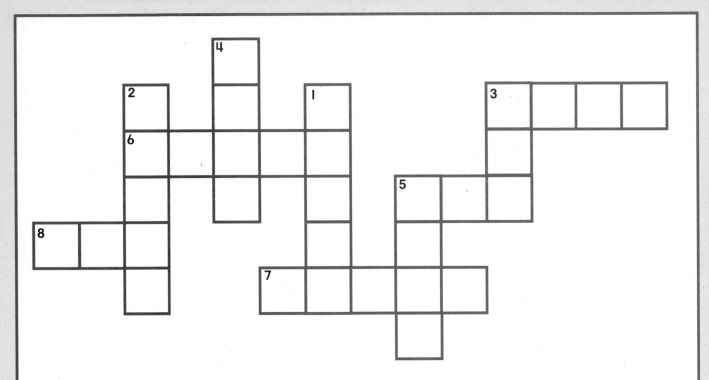

Across

3. What some people's hair can do

5. Something soft and warm

6. The planet we live on

7. Something you wear

8. You can keep many different things in this

Down

1. A fish with sharp teeth

2. A shiny, round stone

3. Something you ride in

4. An animal that lives in a tree

5. A plant with thin, green leaves

Harcourt Brace School Publishers

Name _____

shirt	skirt	farmer	yard	artist	earth	scarf	shark
park	tiger	bird	barn	turtle	writer	teacher	sweater

1 Which are animals?

_____

_____

_____

2 Which are places?

_____

_____

_____

3 Which are things you can wear?

_____

_____

_____

4 Which are people?

_____

_____

_____

Choose the word that answers each riddle. Write the word.

5. I swim in the ocean and have sharp teeth. I am a _____ .

6. I have many trees, flowers, and benches in me. I am a _____ .

7. You wear me. Sometimes I have long sleeves. I am a _____ .

8. I have cows and horses in my barn. I am a _____ .

cloud

flower

Write a word that rhymes with each picture name.

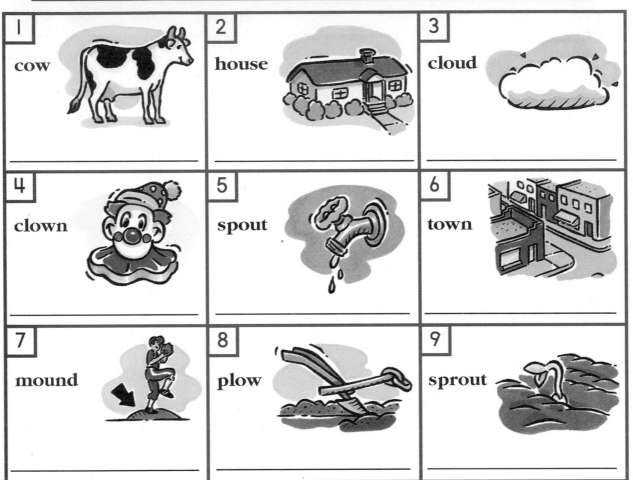

Harcourt Brace School Publishers

Look at the pictures again. Do what the sentences tell you.

10. Draw a bell around the neck of the cow.

11. Draw a flower next to the house.

12. Give the clown a mouth.

Write the word that names each picture.

blouse	towel	couch	plow	crowd	hound

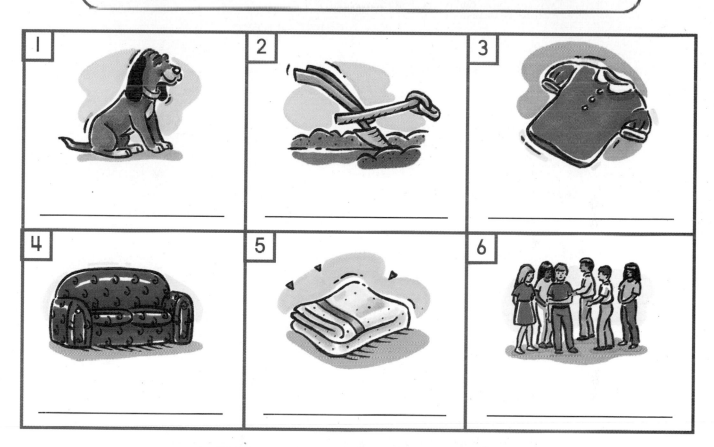

1. _____

2. _____

3. _____

4. _____

5. _____

6. _____

Choose the word that fits each sentence. Write the word.

bow	down	mouse	blouse	south	hour

7. My pet _____ likes to eat cheese.

8. Juan thanked the crowd and then took a _____.

9. Janie wore a brown skirt and a pretty white _____.

10. Artie put his book _____ and went to sleep.

11. Kim can play outdoors for one _____.

12. Eric lives _____ of the lake.

Name _____

Choose the word that answers each riddle. Write the word on the line.

1. Rain falls down from me. I am a _____.
   cloud   clown   club

2. You would like the milk I give! I am a _____.
   couch   cow   cub

3. I have streets and houses. I am a _____.
   ton   towel   town

4. I am funny when I play around. I am a _____.
   clue   cloud   clown

5. I can be found in the ground. I am a _____.
   flower   follow   float

6. Water comes out of me. I am a _____.
   shout   spout   sport

7. I hide when the cat is on the prowl. I am a _____.
   most   mound   mouse

8. You can hear me. I can be soft or loud. I am a _____.
   south   sound   snow

9. When you sit down, you might use me. I am a _____.
   couch   cloud   cube

10. I am proud to rest on the king's head. I am a _____.
    church   crown   crew

11. I can fly down from a tree. I am an _____.
    oil   owl   vowel

12. I am a good pet to have around when something needs to be found. I am a _____.
    hut   house   hound

Phonics Practice Book

Harcourt Brace School Publishers

Read the story and think about what happens.

Lost and Found

For four days the clouds were dark and the rain came down. Mom and I stayed in the house. We watched the raindrops bounce off the ground. We listened to the sounds of the storm.

The next day was sunny. We were invited to go camping with the Brown family. When we got to the camp, my dog Scout jumped out of the car. He ran down the mountain and into some trees.

"How will we ever find him?" I cried. We looked around the area for Scout, but did not see him. He was not to be found!

Then we heard a loud sound in a bush—a dog's howl! It was Scout! I was so glad that we had found him. Well, maybe Scout really found us. He looked so proud.

Write the answers to the questions.

1. What problem did the boy and his mom have at the camp?

_____

2. What happened to Scout?

_____

3. Why did Scout look proud?

_____

Name _____

 <u>c</u>ord   <u>shore</u>   <u>four</u>

Circle the letters that complete the picture name. Write the letters on the line.

1	ore / ire / are	st _____
2	or / ea / er	st __ k _____
3	ou / or / ir	c __ d _____
4	or / ur / ou	st __ m _____
5	or / ea / ar	p __ ch _____
6	or / ou / ar	m __ ning _____
7	ire / our / are	f _____
8	ore / eer / are	c _____
9	ear / our / are	p _____
10	ir / ee / or	t __ n _____
11	oo / or / er	th __ n _____
12	or / er / ar	h __ n _____
13	ore / ur / are	sn _____
14	ar / er / or	c __ n _____
15	or / ou / ar	h __ se _____

R-controlled Vowel: /ôr/*or, ore, our*   Phonics Practice Book

Harcourt Brace School Publishers

d<u>oor</u>

 s<u>oar</u>

Circle the word that completes the sentence. Then write the word.

1. Our family was going to the lake. We locked the front

   _____ and left.

   door   down   done   dirt

2. We were going to use our rowboat. My brother and I each carried

   an _____ .

   oat   oar   oak   oath

3. Near the boat, we saw a hurt bird. Mom said,

   "_____ thing."

   pair   roof   rope   poor

4. We found a box and put the bird in it. "We will help you," we said.

   "Soon you will _____ high in the sky."

   sort   soar   some   soon

5. Soon the bird was better. We saw it hop around on the

   _____ .

   flame   floor   flop   flour

6. We made a ramp for the bird with a _____ .

   board   bread   bore   boat

7. As we watched the bird fly away, we heard a loud sound. "Was that

   a _____ ?" Mom asked.

   roam   road   roar   rear

8. "No, it's just our dog," said my brother. "He's just

   thumping his tail on the _____ ."

   food   floor   fish   for

Name _____

Write the word that names each picture.

clown   house   cord   oar   corn
spout   door   stork   four

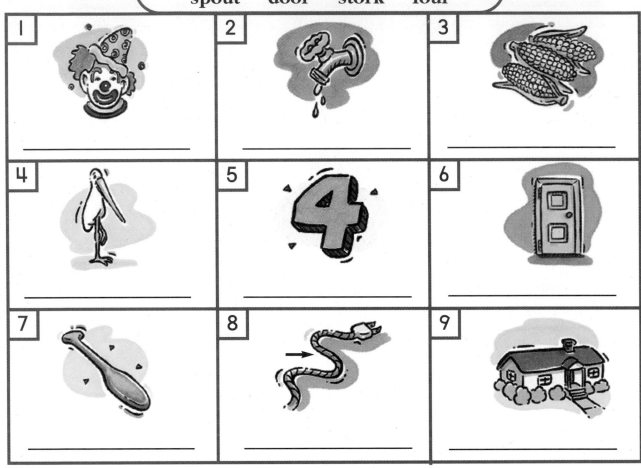

1 _____

2 _____

3 _____

4 _____

5 _____

6 _____

7 _____

8 _____

9 _____

Answer the riddles with words that rhyme. You will not use all of the words.

oar   pour   house   cow

10. What do you say to a farm animal when you want something fast?

"Now, _____!"

11. What do you call the home of a tiny animal that loves cheese?

a mouse _____

12. What do you call a shop that sells paddles?

an _____ store

Review of Diphthong /ou/ow, ou,
R-controlled Vowel: /ôr/or, ore, our, oor, oar

Phonics Practice Book

Name _____

Choose the word that completes each sentence. Then write the word in the puzzle.

| door | four | store | found | cow | town |
| roar | stork | mouse | loud | shore | torn | soar |

ACROSS

2. If you have two pairs of socks, you have _____ socks.

3. We live in a small _____ , not a city.

5. This paper is _____ in half.

6. Will you please open the _____ for me?

9. When we go to the beach, we will play on the _____ .

11. Gail got a new toy at the _____ .

DOWN

1. Did you feed the big brown _____ ?

2. Peter _____ a penny and picked it up.

4. The story is about a tiny white _____ who rides a bike.

7. The lion gave a big _____ .

8. Our teacher says, "Be quiet! You are too _____ ."

9. We saw a plane _____ through the sky.

10. A _____ is a tall bird.

coin

toy

Put a ✔ under each picture whose name has the vowel sound you hear in *coin* and *toy*.

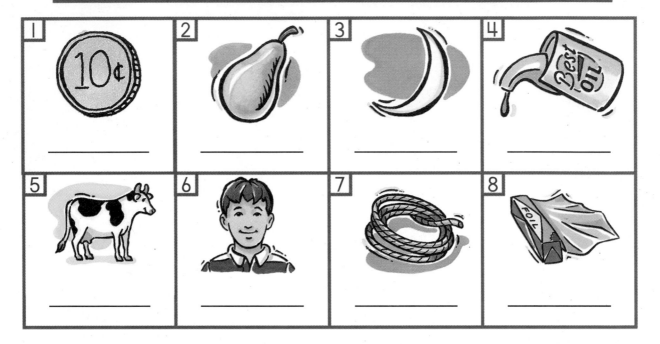

1 _____ 2 _____ 3 _____ 4 _____

5 _____ 6 _____ 7 _____ 8 _____

Circle the word that names the picture. Then write the word on the line.

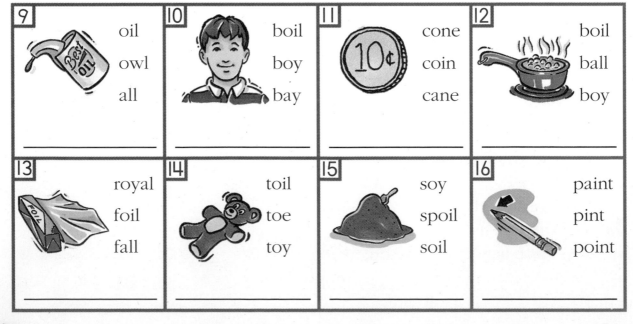

9	oil	10	boil	11	cone	12	boil
	owl		boy		coin		ball
	all		bay		cane		boy

13	royal	14	toil	15	soy	16	paint
	foil		toe		spoil		pint
	fall		toy		soil		point

Vowel Diphthong: /oi/*oi, oy*

Phonics Practice Book

Harcourt Brace School Publishers

Name _____

Write the word that names each picture. You will not use all of the words.

foil	boil	cowboy	coil	toy	soy
soil	point	oil	coin	boy	

1. _____

2. _____

3. _____

4. _____

5. _____

6. _____

7. _____

8. _____

Now use some of the words from above to complete these sentences.

9. I like to play with the _____ next door.

10. Mom let me buy a new _____ to share with him.

11. I chose a little car. It is fast, but it does not need gas or

_____ .

12. I hope my friend will like the car. I used my last _____

to pay for it.

Write a word with *oi* or *oy* to answer each question.

1. What is at the end of a sharp pencil and rhymes with *joint*?

   _____

2. What word names a person who is not a girl? It rhymes with *toy*.

   _____

3. What is another way to cook things that rhymes with *broil*?

   _____

4. What word means "to put things together" and rhymes with *coin*?

   _____

5. What do you call a king and queen and their family? It rhymes with

   loyal. _____

6. What kind of silver paper shines and rhymes with *coil*?

   _____

7. What is a thing to play with that rhymes with *joy*? _____

8. What word names the shape of a rope or a curled-up snake and rhymes

   with *toil*? _____

9. What word means "a little wet" and rhymes with *hoist*?

   _____

10. What word means "happiness" and rhymes with *toy*?

    _____

11. What names something that you can spend or save and rhymes with

    join? _____

12. What do plants grow in? Its name rhymes with *coil*. _____

Vowel Diphthong: /oi/*oi, oy*

Phonics Practice Book

Read the story and answer the questions.

Dad said I could invite a friend to join us for dinner, so I asked my pal Roy. He is the best friend a boy could have. He is smart, funny, and loyal.

When Roy got here, we were hungry. We helped Dad cook dinner. Dad broiled sirloin steak. He put some foil on a pan and sprinkled soy sauce on the steak. He put the sirloin under the broiler. Roy and I snapped fresh beans and put them in a pot to boil. After a while, the steak was done. Dad said it looked nice and moist.

When we sat down to eat, Dad said our meal looked like a royal feast. Did we ever enjoy it! The food was good, and everyone laughed and talked. After we helped Dad clean up, we went to play with my toys. When Roy left, he said he had enjoyed himself. He asked me to join his family for dinner one day soon. Oh, boy!

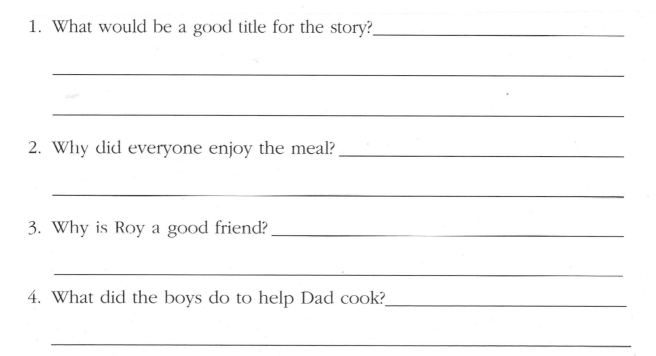

1. What would be a good title for the story?_____

_____

_____

2. Why did everyone enjoy the meal? _____

_____

3. Why is Roy a good friend? _____

_____

4. What did the boys do to help Dad cook?_____

_____

The letters *ou* in *would* and the letters *oo* in *book* stand for the same vowel sound. Write the word that names each picture.

book   brook   hook   wood

1.  _____

2. _____

3. _____

4.  _____

Write *yes* or *no* to answer each question. Then circle each word that has the vowel sound you hear in *cook* and *could*.

5. Should you take a good look before crossing the street?

_____

6. Could a book swim in a brook? _____

7. Would a fishhook fit in a hood? _____

8. Could a coat made of wool keep you warm? _____

9. If you took a log and made a chair, would the chair be made of wood?

_____

10. Could someone cook a fish on a wood fire? _____

11. Should you wear a wool hood to keep cool? _____

Vowel Variant: /o͝o/oo, ou

Name _____

The words below are in the puzzle. Some words go down, and some go across. Find and circle each one.

took	should	look	cookie	foot	would
could	brook	hook	stood	shook	hood
	cook	book	wool	wood	

```
a   b   c   o   o   k   i   e   d   e   w   f   h
s   h   o   u   l   d   d   g   b   r   o   o   k
h   o   u   s   s   v   s   c   o   h   o   l   r
o   o   l   o   o   k   o   c   o   u   l   d   w
o   d   d   b   s   t   o   o   k   l   s   r   o
k   s   v   f   o   o   t   o   h   o   o   k   o
w   o   u   l   d   b   x   k   s   t   o   o   d
```

Write the word from the puzzle that names each picture. You will not use all of the words.

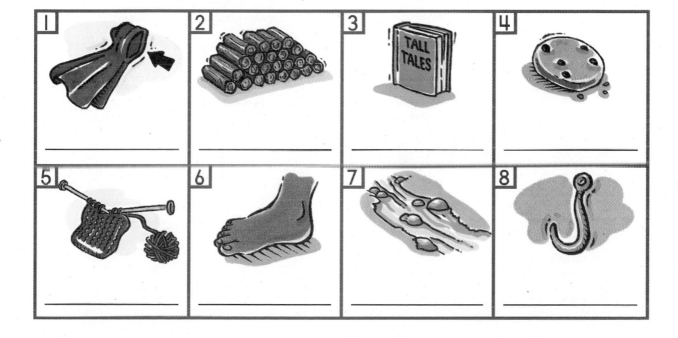

1. _____

2. _____

3. _____

4. _____

5. _____

6. _____

7. _____

8. _____

REVIEW

Do what the sentences tell you.

1. Circle the cowboy's hat.

2. Add a piece of wood to the fire.

3. Draw a small bush in the soil.

4. Mark an X on the coil of rope.

5. Draw a fish in the brook.

Write the word that completes each sentence.

soil   wool   book   broil   look

6. How else could the cowboy cook his food?

    He could _____ it.

7. What could the cowboy do before it gets dark?

    He could read his _____ .

8. What would the cowboy's blanket be made of if it came from a sheep?

    It would be made of _____ .

Review of Vowel Diphthong: /oi/*oi, oy*;
Vowel Variant: /o͞o/*oo, ou* • Reading Words in Context

Phonics Practice Book

Harcourt Brace School Publishers

Name _____

Write the word that names each picture. You will not use all of the words.

| boy | boil | toy | soil | oil | wool | royal | point |
| book | foil | coil | brook | hood | wood | hook |

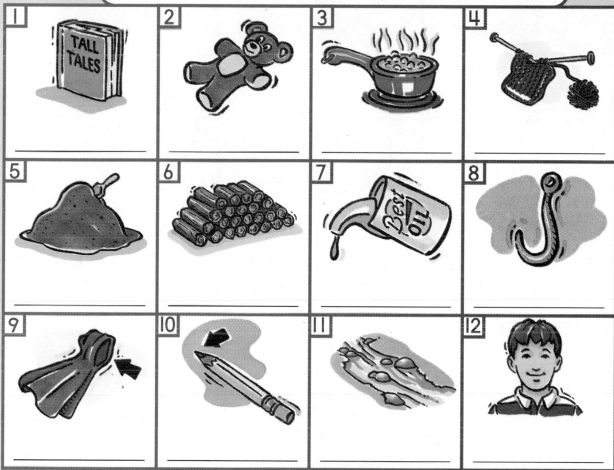

1. TALL TALES _____

2. _____

3. _____

4. _____

5. _____

6. _____

7. _____

8. _____

9. _____

10. _____

11. _____

12. _____

Use some of the words you wrote to complete these sentences:

13. Troy does not want to play with his _____.

14. He wishes he could fish in the _____.

15. He should have brought his pole and _____.

16. Then he would have been a happy _____.

Name _____

Circle the letters that complete each picture name. Then write the letters.

1	er / ir / ar	2	er / oi / ar	3	or / ou / ur
	c _____		tig _____		sp _____

4	ar / oo / ir	5	ear / ir / ar	6	oo / ow / or
	sh _____ t		th _____		cl _____ n

7	oy / or / ou	8	ar / oi / or	9	ar / ear / ore
	h _____ se		w _____ m		st _____

10	our / ear / ow	11	ow / oor / ear	12	ear / ou / oar
	f _____		d _____		s _____

13	ir / oi / oo	14	ou / oo / oy	15	oi / oo / ow
	c _____ n		b _____		b _____ k

Cumulative Review of *R*-controlled Vowels: /är/*ar*; /ûr/*er, ur, ir, ear*;
/ôr/*or, ore, our, oor, oar*; Vowel Diphthong: /ou/*ow, ou*; /oi/*oi, oy*;
Vowel Variant: /ōō/*oo, ou*

Phonics Practice Book

Harcourt Brace School Publishers

Name _____

Circle the name of each picture. Then write the word.

1. card
    curt
    card
    _____

2. shovel
    shopper
    shower
    _____

3. pore
    purse
    power
    _____

4. scarf
    skit
    skirt
    _____

5. earn
    earth
    each
    _____

6. call
    cow
    car
    _____

7. house
    hose
    haze
    _____

8. ham
    horn
    howl
    _____

9. star
    stir
    store
    _____

10. four
    far
    fir
    _____

11. deep
    day
    door
    _____

12. oak
    oar
    oats
    _____

13. oil
    oar
    order
    _____

14. box
    boy
    bay
    _____

15. bark
    beak
    book
    _____

Cumulative Review of *R*-controlled Vowels: /är/*ar*; /ûr/*er, ur, ir, ear*; /ôr/*or, ore, our, oor, oar*; Vowel Diphthong: /ou/*ow, ou*; /oi/*oi, oy*; Vowel Variant: /o͞o/*oo, ou*

Harcourt Brace School Publishers

beard

deer

Circle the word that completes the sentence.
Write the word on the line.

1. Today was to be the biggest day of the _____.

    your   yard   year

2. Our team had a game. We had all our _____ ready.

    gear   germ   grow

3. When I got up, I could _____ a noise.

    hear   hair   hurt

4. I went to _____ outside to see what it was.

    peer   park   pour

5. I had a _____ that it was rain, and I was right.

    fair   fear   fir

6. I called a friend who lives _____ me.

    now   near   need

7. While we were talking, she let out a _____.

    cheat   cheer   chair

8. She had looked outside and seen a young _____.

    deer   dart   dent

9. "What a _____ little animal!" she said, as he ran off.

    dare   dial   dear

10. Soon the rain stopped, and the sky grew _____.
    We could play our game!   clear   clerk   claim

Circle the name of each picture. Then write the word.

1
shares
stairs
starts

_____

2
spare
part
pear

_____

3
mare
mint
main

_____

4
hang
hire
hare

_____

5
heat
hate
hair

_____

6
bear
beast
beard

_____

7
tart
tear
target

_____

8
barn
bare
bake

_____

9
share
shack
shirt

_____

10
chart
chair
chain

_____

11
square
spray
squire

_____

12
earn
air
aim

_____

Read the story and think about what happens.

We have pear trees on our farm. In the winter the trees are bare. In the spring they have flowers that make the air smell nice. In the summer the trees are full of pears. When the trees have pears, my friend and I help pick them.

We get up on chairs to reach the pears. We pick all we can reach. I save a few for Clair, my mare. My friend gives some to his pet hare, Carey. We walk back to the house and sit on the stairs to eat our good, sweet pears.

Write the answers to the questions.

1. What would be a good title for the story?

_____

2. How do the trees change during the year?

_____

_____

3. Who eats the pears?

_____

R-controlled Vowel: /âr/*air, ear, are* • Reading Words in Context

Phonics Practice Book

Name _____

Read the sentences and do what they tell you.

1. Write the year under the words *State Fair*.

2. Circle what the girl will wear.

3. Draw a line under those who give a cheer.

4. Put an X on the mare.

5. Draw a pair of eyeglasses on the girl.

6. Put a big dot near the steer.

7. Mark a check (✔) over the man with a beard.

8. Put a box around the boy near the steer.

9. Write *deer* on the deer's pen.

10. Draw leaves on the bare tree.

Harcourt Brace School Publishers

REVIEW | **Read the poem, and answer the questions.**

The Camping Trip

The air is crisp.
The sky is fair.
We drive from the city
Without a care.

We unpack our gear,
Our tent big and square.
I've broken a chair,
But Mom packed a spare.

We dare the dark woods,
Just hoping to see
A soft, little hare
Or a deer wild and free.

We break up our camp,
For school days are near.
We are sad to go home,
But we'll come back next year!

Harcourt Brace School Publishers

1. What is the weather like for the trip?

   _____

2. What do the campers hope to see in the woods?

   _____

3. Why are there still enough chairs?

   _____

Review of R-controlled Vowels: /ir/ *ear, eer*; /âr/ *air, ear, are*   Phonics Practice Book

flew

blue

Write an *ew* or a *ue* word to answer each question.

1. What is a color that rhymes with *glue?* _____

2. What can help you solve a mystery? It rhymes with *true.*

   _____

3. What word tells what you do to your food and rhymes with *threw?*

   _____

4. What can you eat with a spoon that rhymes with *few?*

   _____

5. What do you call a team of people who work together?

   with *grew.* _____

Complete each sentence with an *ew* or a *ue* word.

6. My sister lost her ring. She did not have a _____ where to find it.

7. She said, "I had it when I was helping Dad make _____ for supper."

8. "Maybe you threw it out with the peels in the _____ trash bag," I said.

9. "That must be it!" she said. We ran home to check the bag before the garbage _____ picked it up.

Circle the word that answers each riddle. Write the word on the line.

1. I am the color of the sky on a bright, clear day. I am _____.

    bloom   blue   blank

2. When you do not know something, I help you find it out. I am a

    _____.

    chew   clue   coop

3. I am a boy, and I have an aunt. I am her _____.

    nephew   noon   next

4. I make things stick to paper. I am _____.

    glare   gleam   glue

5. You can walk down me because I am like a street. I am an _____.

    afternoon   avenue   animal

6. I am a special kind of stone you can wear. I am a _____.

    jewel   jeep   juice

7. I am a thick soup with carrots, potatoes, and meat. I am a

    _____.

    stew   stool   street

8. When you read me, I tell you about things that have happened.

    I am the _____.

    near   news   noise

Vowel Variant: /o͞o/ue, ew

Phonics Practice Book

Harcourt Brace School Publishers

Read the book titles. Look for words that have the vowel sound you hear in the words *grew* and *glue*. Then write the words under the correct heading.

Words with *ew* like *grew*

_____

_____

_____

Words that end with *ue*, like *glue*

_____

_____

_____

Write the answers to the questions.

1. Which book probably has many stories in it?

_____

2. Which book is a mystery?

_____

3. Which book is not a fantasy?

_____

Name _____

fawn   taught   bought

Write the word that names each picture.

caught   lawn   yawn   crawl   paw   hawk

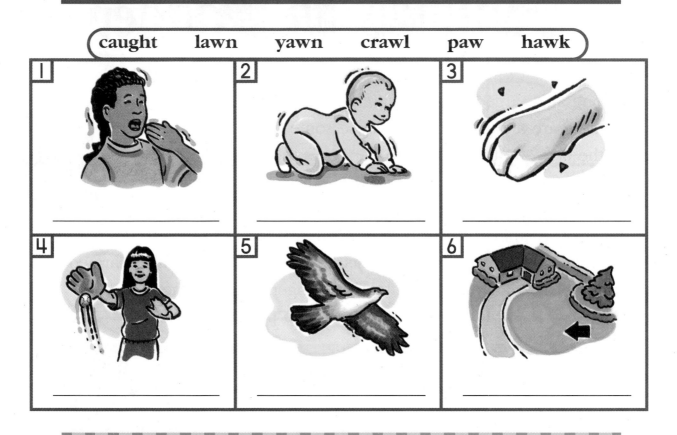

1. _____

2. _____

3. _____

4. _____

5. _____

6. _____

Circle the word that the sentence tells about.

7. If you grabbed a ball from the air, you could say you did this.

    caught   call   could

8. If you are tired, you might do this with your mouth.

    yard   yawn   yellow

9. If someone helped you learn something, they did this.

    tweak   tooth   taught

10. If someone feels that you should do something, they might use this word in telling you about it.

    oat   ought   odd

Vowel Variant: /ô/aw, au(gh), ou(gh)

Phonics Practice Book

Harcourt Brace School Publishers

Write *yes* or *no* to answer each question.

1. Does a goldfish have a claw? _____

2. Can a hawk play the piano? _____

3. Should you yawn during dinner? _____

4. Do bunnies have soft paws? _____

5. Can a fawn fly in the sky? _____

6. Should you let a rhino on your lawn? _____

Choose the word that completes each sentence. Write the word.

7. My sister Dawn and I went to the river to go fishing. We saw a

    _____ with a fluffy, white tail.

    fawn   found   fan

8. We usually do not agree on the kind of fishing bait to use, but we have

    never _____ about it.

    fruit   fought   foot

9. Dawn must have chosen the right bait, because she _____

    the fish.

    cow   crow   caught

10. We did not stay a long time. We had gotten up early, and I started to

    _____.

    yawn   yard   yarn

Vowel Variant: /ô/aw, au(gh), ou(gh)   173

Read the story, and think about what happens.

The Surprise in the Woods

Grandpa and I got up at dawn and went into the woods. We wanted to see some animals. We thought we might see some birds and a few squirrels. Were we ever surprised by what we saw!

When we sat down for a rest, I saw something moving in the trees. I was not sure what it was. Then I knew. It was a bear! It had long, sharp claws, and big, strong jaws. I told Grandpa we ought to go. Just then, the bear ran away. Was I ever glad! That bear taught me that I ought to be careful when I'm in the woods.

Write the answers to the questions.

1. Why did the boy and his grandpa go into the woods?

_____

2. What surprising thing did they see?

_____

3. What happened that made the boy glad?

_____

Harcourt Brace School Publishers

Look at the picture. Then follow the directions.

He _____ it!

1. Circle the person who is learning to crawl.

2. The baby has just caught a ball. Draw the ball in his hands.

3. Draw a line under the person who has taught the baby to catch.

4. Finish the mother's thought.

5. Put an X on the new thing the mother bought for the baby.

6. Circle the thing the mother ought to give the baby when he is hungry.

7. Draw a pillow in the place where the mother will put the baby when he begins to yawn.

8. Circle the puppy's paws.

9. Draw a window in the room that shows the front lawn.

Harcourt Brace School Publishers

REVIEW

Write the word that names each picture.

bought	crawl	caught	hammer	taught
zipper	salad	fawn	table	thousand
sofa	thought	straw	puzzle	butter

1	2	3
_____	_____	_____

4	5	6
_____	_____	_____

7	8	9
_____	_____	_____

10	11	12
_____	_____	_____

13	14	15
_____	_____	_____

Review: Schwa; Vowel Variant: /ô/aw, au(gh), ou(gh)

Phonics Practice Book

Use the rhyming words to complete the poem.

caught	stronger	thought	able
taught	ago	crawl	

1. Have you ever heard the fable about the turtle who was

   _____ ?

2. Very, very long _____ , Turtle and Hare's race was
   the show.

3. Hare said speediness can't be _____ , it can't be
   promised or be bought.

4. But Turtle did not give up at all and moved along at a steady

   _____ .

5. "Since I have time, I think I ought to take a nap right here,"

   Hare _____ .

6. Turtle kept it up much longer and proved that he was really

   _____ .

7. In the end, Hare had been taught that Turtle now could not be

   _____ !

Review: Schwa; Vowel Variant: /ô/ aw, au(gh), ou(gh)

Name _____

Circle the word that names the picture. Then write the word.

1	beard beast bread _____	2	chair cheer chore _____	3	suit soon soup _____

4	mean main moon _____	5	chain cheer chair _____	6	table tickle towel _____

7	peer pear people _____	8	straw stream stray _____	9	sought squirm square _____

10	cut caught couple _____	11	fruit fry fright _____	12	boot bite bought _____

13	flea flew flow _____	14	butter battle button _____	15	glow glue group _____

Harcourt Brace School Publishers

Cumulative Review: /ir/ear, eer; /âr/air, ear, are;
 /o͞o/ue, ew, oo, ou, ui; /ə/a, /əl/le, /ər/er; /ô/aw, augh, ough

Name _____

Look at the picture. Then follow the directions.

1. Write *We Care About Deer* at the top of one poster.
2. Draw an arrow pointing to the person who taught the class about animals.
3. Draw a zebra on another poster.
4. Draw a jar of glue on a desk.
5. Draw a bicycle on the playground.
6. Write the year in the date on the board.
7. Draw a few more fish in the tank.

Harcourt Brace School Publishers

Phonics Practice Book

Cumulative Review of /ir/*ear, eer;* /âr/*air, ear, are;*
/o͞o/*ue, ew, oo, ou, ui;* /ə/*a,* /əl/ */le,/ər/er;* /ô/*aw, au(gh), ou(gh)*

179

Name _____

Fill in the circle next to the word that names the picture.

1
- ○ thunder
- ○ table
- ○ tear

2
- ○ dare
- ○ door
- ○ deer

3
- ○ crawl
- ○ caught
- ○ cough

4
- ○ glow
- ○ good
- ○ glue

5
- ○ bar
- ○ bear
- ○ bead

6
- ○ chop
- ○ chair
- ○ cheer

7
- ○ salad
- ○ sled
- ○ sleet

8
- ○ skip
- ○ squid
- ○ square

9
- ○ tight
- ○ taught
- ○ tooth

10
- ○ water
- ○ waddle
- ○ whistle

11
- ○ hare
- ○ hire
- ○ hear

12
- ○ thousand
- ○ thought
- ○ taught

13
- ○ jungle
- ○ jewel
- ○ jacket

14
- ○ sports
- ○ spoke
- ○ spoon

15
- ○ seat
- ○ suit
- ○ sight

16
- ○ threat
- ○ thought
- ○ those

180

Test: /ir/*ear, eer;* /âr/*air, ear, are;*
/o͞o/*ue, ew, oo, ou, ui;* /ə/*a,* /əl/*le,* /ər/*er;* /ô/*aw, au(gh), ou(gh)*

Fill in the circle next to the sentence that tells about the picture.

1	○ The children wish they could get into the water. ○ The children wish they could use a hammer. ○ The children wish they could read a letter.
2	○ They fear the water. ○ They get their gear. ○ They look under the car.
3	○ They thought the sky was clear and blue, but then they saw clouds. ○ They saw a hawk in the clear blue sky. ○ They caught sight of a plane in the clear, blue sky.
4	○ The wind blew their hair. ○ The wind blew over a chair. ○ The wind did not blow.
5	○ They got caught in a river. ○ They got caught in a rain shower. ○ They were taught how to swim.
6	○ They were dry because they wore their coats. ○ They got wet, though not in the pool. ○ They got wet at school.
7	○ They agreed to wait for a while. ○ They were able to swim in the water. ○ They agreed to put a puzzle together.
8	○ The children gave a cheer when the sun came out. ○ The children did not care when the sun came out. ○ The children stood on chairs when the sun came out.

Test: /ir/ear, eer; /âr/air, ear, are; /o͞o/ue, ew, oo, ou, ui; /ə/a, /əl/le, /ər/er; /ô/aw, au(gh), ou(gh)   **181**

Name _____

 snail   **smile**   **scoop**

When two consonants come together in a word, you usually blend together the sounds they stand for. Write the word that names the picture.

scout	scarf	snow	scale
smock	smoke	scarecrow	sneaker
snout	snake	score	smile

1 _____

2 _____

3 _____

4 _____

5 _____

6 _____

7 _____

8 _____

9 _____

10 _____

11 _____

12 _____

stamp

skate

spoon

Answer each question with a word that begins with *st, sk,* or *sp*.

1. What belongs on a letter and rhymes with *damp*? _____

2. What has eight legs and rhymes with *rider*? _____

3. What do you see when you go outside and look up? It rhymes with *fly*.

    _____

4. What do clowns walk on to look very tall? They rhyme with *tilts*.

    _____

5. What covers your body and rhymes with *tin*? _____

6. What means "to begin" and rhymes with *part*? _____

7. What animal gives off a strong smell and rhymes with *bunk*?

    _____

8. What do you walk up to go from the first floor to the second floor? It

    rhymes with *chairs.* _____

9. What can a toy top do? It rhymes with *tin*. _____

10. What is another name for a small rock? It rhymes with *bone.*

    _____

Name _____

 bread   **crab**   **grapes**   **frog**   **dragon**   **train**   **pretzel**

Circle the word that names the picture. Then write the word.

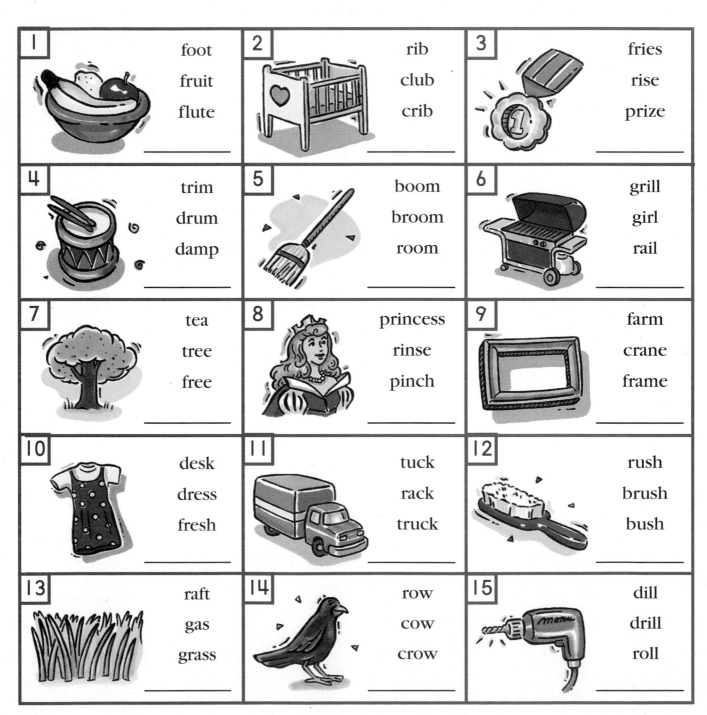

1 foot / fruit / flute _____	**2** rib / club / crib _____	**3** fries / rise / prize _____
4 trim / drum / damp _____	**5** boom / broom / room _____	**6** grill / girl / rail _____
7 tea / tree / free _____	**8** princess / rinse / pinch _____	**9** farm / crane / frame _____
10 desk / dress / fresh _____	**11** tuck / rack / truck _____	**12** rush / brush / bush _____
13 raft / gas / grass _____	**14** row / cow / crow _____	**15** dill / drill / roll _____

Initial Clusters with *r*   Phonics Practice Book

Harcourt Brace School Publishers

Name _____

The words below are in the puzzle. Some words go down and some words go across. Find and circle each one.

branch   crab   grill   crown   pretzel
brush   cry   dragon   train   prize

P	R	E	T	Z	E	L	B
R	Y	C	R	O	W	N	R
I	D	R	A	G	O	N	A
Z	G	R	I	L	L	Z	N
E	R	X	N	C	R	Y	C
C	R	A	B	R	U	S	H

Write the word from the puzzle that names each picture.

1. _____

2. _____

3. _____

4. _____

5. _____

6. _____

7. _____

8. _____

9. _____

10. _____

When two consonants come together in a word, you usually blend together the sounds they stand for. Write the letters that complete each picture name.

blocks   **clover**   **planet**   **flag**

1 ____ ock	2 ____ ag	3 ____ um
4 ____ ouse	5 ____ y	6 ____ ate
7 ____ ame	8 ____ anket	9 ____ oud
10 ____ am	11 ____ ug	12 ____ ack

Harcourt Brace School Publishers

Name _____

Follow the directions below the picture.

1. Circle the club member who is climbing the ladder.

2. Write *Club* on the sign over the door.

3. Draw a pretty blossom on the tree.

4. Add a smoke trail behind the plane that is flying in the sky.

5. Draw blinds on the window.

6. Draw a fluffy cloud over the sun in the sky.

7. Draw a flag on top of the roof.

8. Circle the pail of plums on the floor.

9. Draw a folded blanket on the porch.

Name _____

 <u>swan</u>

 <u>twins</u>

Circle the word that names the picture.
Write the word on the line.

1	wig
	twig
	tug
_____

2	win
	sum
	swim
_____

3	stitch
	which
	switch
_____

4	twenty
	swimming
	wrinkle
_____

5	sing
	swing
	wing
_____

6	well
	tells
	twelve
_____

Write the word that completes each sentence. You will not use all the words.

swam	twice	twinkle	twin
tweet	sweater	sweep	sweet

7. Kim likes to eat _____ apples.

8. Fred's pet bird can only say, "_____."

9. Sue looks just like her _____ sister.

10. On cool days Joe wears a _____.

11. Will you help me _____ the floor?

12. Ruth went to the zoo _____ last week.

Name _____

Write the word that begins with *sw* or *tw* that answers each question.

1. What means "very fast" and rhymes with *lift*? _____

2. What is a way to clean up that rhymes with *creep*? _____

3. What sound from a bird rhymes with *feet*? _____

4. What means "more than once" and rhymes with *nice*? _____

5. What is something on a playground that rhymes with *king*?

    _____

6. What might a dancer do that rhymes with *girl*? _____

7. What turns things on and off and rhymes with *ditch*? _____

8. What do you call sisters or brothers born at the same time? It rhymes

    with *pins*. _____

9. What do you do to a jar lid that rhymes with *wrist*? _____

10. What way to move in water rhymes with *him*? _____

11. What is ten plus ten? It rhymes with *plenty*. _____

12. What word tells how honey tastes? It rhymes with *street*. _____

Name _____

Write the letters that complete each picture name.

1 ile	**2** um	**3** ab
4 ider	**5** oom	**6** im
7 ocks	**8** ow	**9** ig
10 ute	**11** ain	**12** amp
13 um	**14** am	**15** unk

Harcourt Brace School Publishers

Name _____

Snow flurries started to fall early on Tuesday. Soon snowflakes covered everything. We were pleased when our teacher sent us home early. We were not scared of a little snow.

"Hooray!" we yelled as we skidded home on the ice.

At first we just watched the blizzard from the window. The sparkling snow looked so pretty.

On Wednesday the snow was still blowing around. It piled in drifts in front of the door. We could not even clean off the sidewalk. When we opened the door, a blast of swirling snow blew in. The schools were closed. We watched some TV. Then we played some games. Our first snow day had been fun. But by Wednesday evening we felt a little bored.

On Thursday we were just plain crabby. We were tired of snowflakes swirling and twirling. They did not look pretty any more. We were tired of freezing breezes blowing around us. We were tired of being closed up in the house.

On Friday morning the bright sun climbed into a blue sky. No more blizzard! We felt free. We all smiled. Believe it or not, it felt great to be going back to school. We could not wait to see our friends.

1. How did the children feel about the snow on Tuesday?

_____

2. How did the children feel when it was time to go back to school? Why?

_____

_____

scratch   strawberry   spray   squirrel

Write the word from the box that answers each question.

square   stream   spring   scrub   string   street   strike
scrap   scream   stranger   squid   spread

1. What is a season of the year? _____

2. What is something you do to a dirty floor? _____

3. What word for a little river rhymes with *team*? _____

4. What is a place for driving cars? _____

5. What is something you tie onto a kite? _____

6. What is a shape that rhymes with *rare?* _____

7. What is something left over that rhymes with *map*?

    _____

8. Who is a person you do not know? _____

9. What is something you can do with jelly? It rhymes with *head*.

    _____

10. What is a sea animal that rhymes with *lid*? _____

11. What is a word for a loud yell? _____

12. What word means "a swing that misses the ball"? _____

Harcourt Brace School Publishers

Circle the word that completes the sentence. Write the word on the line.

1

spring
ring
string

It is a warm day in _____.

2

scrapbooks
scatter
strawberries

Casey plants _____.

3

scrapes
soaps
straps

First she _____ away the weeds.

4

pouts
spots
sprouts

Then she plants the _____ in the ground.

5

sports
squirts
spreads

She _____ water on the new plants.

6

straw
trees
saw

She covers them with _____.

7

sting
song
string

She makes a fence with _____.

8

strap
scrub
sub

She will _____ her hands before she eats the berries.

Initial Clusters: *scr, str, spr, squ*

193

Follow the directions. Write the new word. Then draw a picture of it.

1 Start with *wash*. Change *w* to *squ*.	_____	
2 Start with *wipe*. Change *w* to *str.*	_____	
3 Start with *green*. Change the *gr* to *scr*.	_____	
4 Start with *hare*. Change *h* to *squ*.	_____	
5 Start with *sing*. Change *s* to *spr*.	_____	
6 Start with *bring*. Change *br* to *str*.	_____	

Initial Clusters: *scr, str, spr, squ*

Harcourt Brace School Publishers

Name _____

Read the poem. Then write the answers to the questions.

The Big Game

We sprint to the field.
The crowd gives a scream.
We are strong, we are mighty—
The number one team.

We spring up so high
To catch every ball.
We watch the other team—
Squirm, squeal, and sprawl.

By the end of the game,
We're scruffy and dirty,
But we feel no stress—
The score is zero to thirty.

Bright streamers are flying.
Winning is fun!
We've stretched out our streak
And are still number ONE!

1. How do the players feel at the end of the game? Why?

   _____

   _____

2. Write a headline about the game for the team scrapbook.

   _____

   _____

nest

paint

belt

gift

Write the word that completes each sentence.

adult	best	breakfast	cent	cost	elephant
feast	gift	hunt	rent	just	want

1. I _____ you to come to my birthday party.

2. Eat only a small _____ in the morning.

3. Lunch will be a real _____ !

4. After lunch we will _____ for hidden prizes.

5. You might want to _____ or make a costume.

6. Joe wants to make an _____ costume.

7. I think that will _____ too much.

8. I do not want to spend one _____ .

9. I might _____ come as a mouse.

10. Tell your mom that an _____ will be in charge.

11. We will have the _____ time ever!

12. Oh, I almost forgot. Do not bring a birthday _____ .

Final Clusters with *t: st, nt, lt, ft*

Phonics Practice Book

Harcourt Brace School Publishers

Circle the word that fits the clue.

1. You eat this in the morning.
   bolt   breakfast   bent

2. This can be used to lock your door.
   bush   bolt   ball

3. You do this with a pencil to make letters or words.
   pest   prize   print

4. This means a pile of snow blown by the wind.
   drill   drift   dent

5. This is a horse's baby.
   cold   colt   cart

6. This means "the land next to an ocean."
   coast   coat   cone

7. This is the opposite of right.
   list   laugh   left

8. This often goes with pepper.
   sift   sail   salt

9. This has a trunk but never packs it.
   eleven   telephone   elephant

10. You may do this to a cake after you bake it.
    frost   fish   flat

11. This is something you might float on in a lake.
    raft   rent   roof

12. This is not the back.
    from   front   frog

Name _____

 milk   desk   wasp   gold   lamp   band

Write the letters that complete each word.

1. ju _____	2. ha _____	3. sta _____
4. mi _____	5. ba _____	6. de _____
7. bli _____	8. chi _____	9. ca _____
10. po _____	11. du _____	12. ma _____
13. sa _____	14. wa _____	15. ra _____

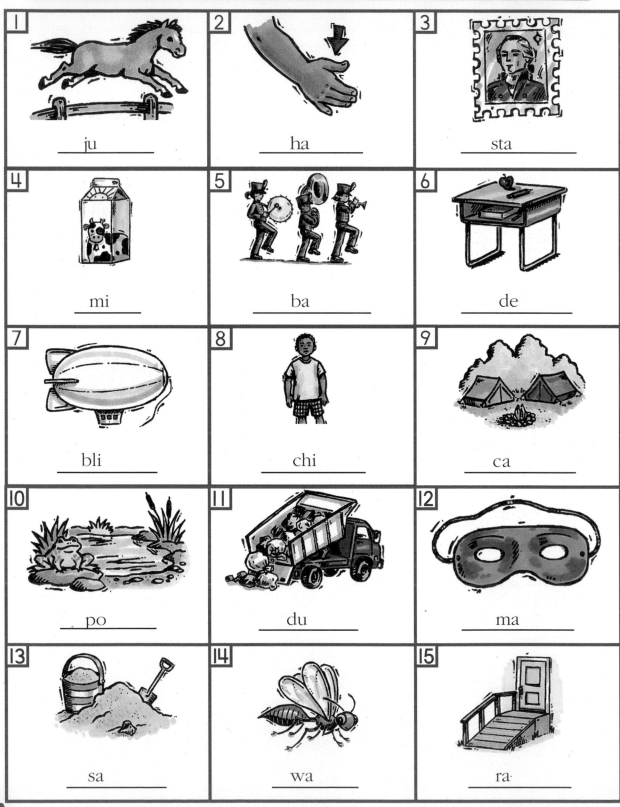

Final Clusters: *lk, sk, sp, ld, mp, nd*

Harcourt Brace School Publishers

Name _____

Come to the Farm!

Are you tired of sitting at a desk all day? Then spend this summer at the Romp family's farm. See what it is like to work on the land.

You will be outside in the brisk, crisp air all day. You can work in the field with Mr. Romp. You can husk corn or milk a cow in the barn. You can pull a clump of weeds or pick plump, ripe apples in the orchard. You can join in on any household task you like. Do not be afraid to ask questions. By the end of your stay, you will understand how a farm really works.

When each day's work is done, it is time to have some fun. You can attend a band concert in town or swim in the pond. You can look for wild animal tracks in the woods. You may even make a new friend or two.

Write the answers to the questions.

1. Where is a good place to spend the summer?

   _____

2. What task can you do in the barn?_____

   _____

3. What task can you do in the orchard? _____

   _____

4. Where can you swim after the work is done? _____

   _____

REVIEW | Write the word that completes each sentence.

cold colt dent desk elk left
raft scrap string stripe toast wasp

1. Jane had orange juice, _____, and cereal for breakfast.

2. A baby horse is called a _____.

3. The _____ has large antlers.

4. Be careful. The _____ may sting!

5. Leroy likes to float on a _____ in his pool.

6. The art teacher made a puppet from a _____ of cloth.

7. We tied a _____ to the kite.

8. A skunk has a _____ on its back.

9. The computer is on the _____.

10. Turn _____ at the next street.

11. The car has a _____ on the side.

12. It is too _____ to swim.

Review of Consonant Clusters

Phonics Practice Book

Harcourt Brace School Publishers

Circle the word that completes the sentence. Write the word on the line.

1		The squid lives in the _____ waters of the ocean.	coal call cold
2		The squid can _____ a jet of water from its head.	scrap sit squirt
3		The jet makes it _____ through the water.	soap spring sit
4		It jets around to _____ for food.	hunt hut him
5		The squid has ten arms but not one _____ .	hen had hand
6		A squid squirts ink to hide in so its enemies can't _____ it.	fall find fill
7		It can _____ away inside its cloud of ink.	dot date drift

city

cow

When *c* is followed by *e*, *i*, or *y*, the *c* usually stands for the sound at the beginning of *city*. When *c* is followed by other letters, it usually stands for the sound at the beginning of *cow*.
Write the word that names each picture.

cents	center	cereal	computer
camera	corn	cabin	cymbal
celery	camel	comb	ceiling

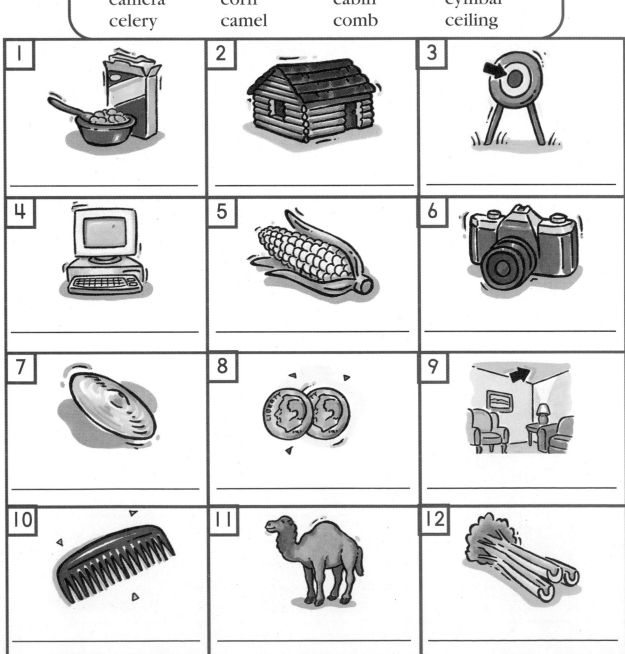

1

2

3

4

5

6

7

8

9

10

11

12

Circle the soft *c* word that best finishes each sentence. Write it on the line.

1	Centerville will _____ its centennial.	celebrate enjoying calling
2	This means that the _____ is 100 years old.	candy town city
3	Centerville is _____ to have a big party.	contain certain sure
4	The _____ will get together.	people cousins citizens
5	They will come to the _____ of town.	center candle middle
6	A _____ will make a speech.	calendar celebrity star

Initial Soft *c* 203

Write the hard *c* words to complete the rhyme.

cackle   cat   cocoon   cold
colt   couch   cover   cow

When the leaves turn gold, and the days grow _____ ,

When wood fires crackle, and starlings _____ ,

Animals may discover it is time to take _____ .

Caterpillar will sleep soon in its warm _____ .

Mouse will say, "Ouch!" and hide under the _____ .

"To the barn I must bolt," says the frisky _____ .

"Where is my green grass now?" complains the _____ .

"I will lie here and grow fat," purrs the warm, cozy _____ .

Write the answers to the questions.

1. What season is the poem about?

    _____

2. Why do the animals need to take cover?

    _____

Harcourt Brace School Publishers

Initial Hard *c*

Phonics Practice Book

Name _____

Cindy loves to cook. So does her brother, Carl. One day they got out their old cookbook. They looked at the recipes— Celery Salad, Country Ham, Corn on the Cob, and Candied Yams.

"Ugh!" said Carl. "We have tried every recipe here. This cookbook is boring."

"You are certainly right!" answered Cindy. "I have an idea. We can make something new. We can make up our own cookbook."

So they did. Here is the table of contents for their new cookbook:

Cucumber Candy 1	Cement Cookies 5
Centipede Stew 2	Cedar Cereal 6

1. What recipes were in the old cookbook?

_____

2. Why did the children make a new cookbook?

_____

_____

3. Which of the new recipes would you be willing to try?

_____

Circle the word that names each picture. Then write the word.

1.
package
palace
parka

_____

2.
fender
fork
fence

_____

3.
itchy
inch
icy

_____

4.
fancy
flock
fiction

_____

5.
piece
pack
pets

_____

6.
polite
police
pails

_____

7.
mike
mice
music

_____

8.
rack
rust
race

_____

9.
juice
jacket
join

_____

10.
space
speak
sports

_____

11.
lake
lace
lack

_____

12.
slide
slice
slick

_____

13.
bound
bow
bounce

_____

14.
praise
price
press

_____

15.
face
fact
fair

_____

Harcourt Brace School Publishers

Name _____

1. Draw a box of supplies in the canoe.

2. Write *Camp Cardinal* on the sign.

3. Find a word that means "money" and circle it.

4. Draw smoke coming from the cabin's chimney.

5. Mark an X on the candle and cup on the picnic table.

6. Circle the cat in the window.

7. Draw logs for the cabin walls.

8. Mark an X in the center of the door.

9. Draw some corn on the cob on the plate.

10. Add some buttons to the camper's coat.

Now circle each soft *c* word and underline each hard *c* word in the directions.

Harcourt Brace School Publishers

When *g* is followed by *e, y,* or *i*, it often stands for the soft sound heard at the beginning of *gem*. When *g* is followed by other letters, it usually stands for the hard sound heard at the beginning of *golf*.

Write the word that names each picture. You will not use all the words.

gem

golf

gift	gym	girl	gem	giraffe	goose	gull	goat
garden	game	gymnast	giant	goose	gerbil	gum	gorilla

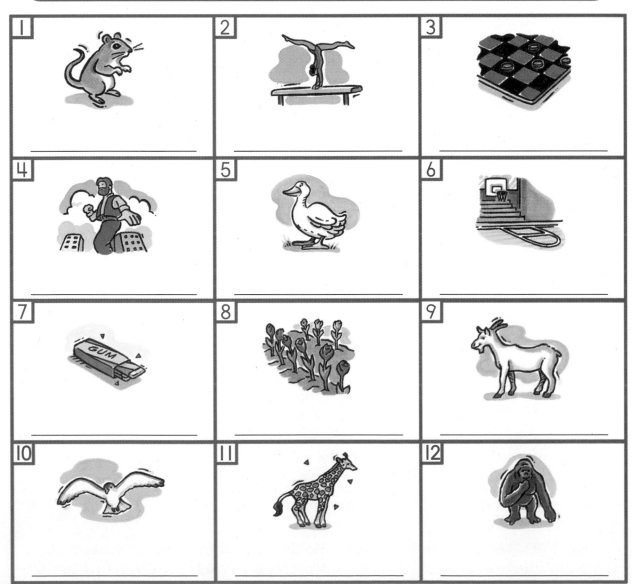

1.

2.

3.

4.

5.

6.

7.

8.

9.

10.

11.

12.

Circle the soft *g* word that completes each sentence. Then write the word on the line.

1	My friend is a very good _____ .	gentleman gymnast jumper
2	She is not tall, but she leaps as high as a _____ would.	germ pony giant
3	Every _____ she makes is graceful.	general movement gesture
4	When she performs in meets, she sparkles like a _____ .	center gem general
5	Sometimes I visit the _____ with her.	gym gentle mall
6	My friend is so small that next to her, I feel like a _____ !	tumbler gym giraffe

Write the hard *g* word that completes each rhyme.

Gail	gallery	gas	gate
goat	gobble	gorilla	guppy

1. A purple raincoat

   Would look odd on a _____.

2. When you need to pass,

   Just step on the _____.

3. A painting by Valerie

   Hangs in the art _____.

4. I asked for a puppy.

   Mom got me a _____.

5. Turkeys walk with a wobble.

   Then they stop and say "_____."

6. The sailor told a tale

   Of a pale whale named _____.

7. If you plan to be late,

   We won't lock the _____.

8. "Chocolate or vanilla?"

   Sam asked the _____.

Harcourt Brace School Publishers

Read the story, and answer the questions.

Gentle Ginger

Ginger is a pretty dog. She got her name because she is a golden retriever. Many dogs just gulp down their meals and play games all day, but not Ginger. She goes to school. When she finishes school, she will go to live with Gina, who uses a wheelchair. She will help out in her new home.

At first, school was hard for Ginger. She had to learn many commands and gestures. She learned to get things for Gina and even how to open a gate. She was taught to be gentle and not to gallop around while she is working.

Now Ginger lives with Gina. Gina thinks Ginger is a genius. But Gina is good at learning, too. She has learned how to make work seem like a game to Ginger. The best part is that Gina and Ginger are good friends.

1. How did Ginger learn to help Gina?

_____

2. Name two things Ginger does to help Gina.

_____

3. What does Gina think of Ginger?

_____

Name _____

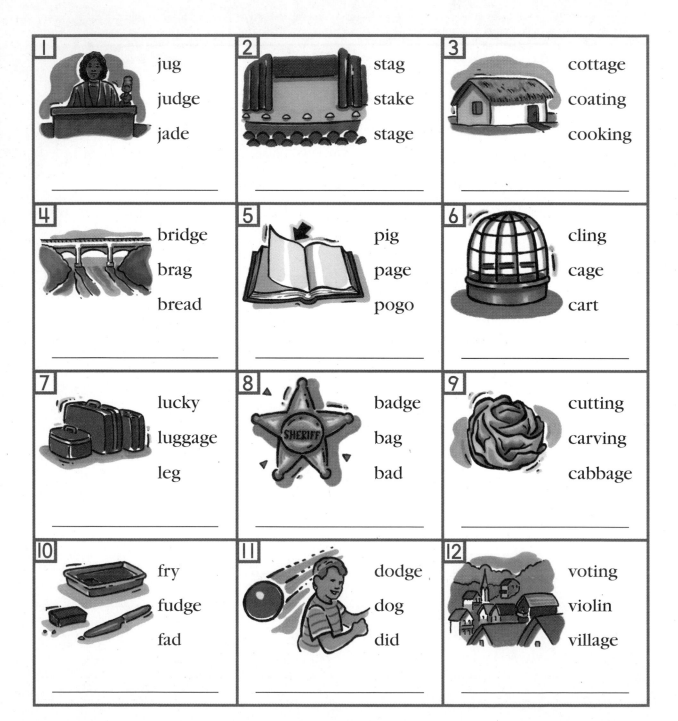

1. jug
   judge
   jade
   _____

2. stag
   stake
   stage
   _____

3. cottage
   coating
   cooking
   _____

4. bridge
   brag
   bread
   _____

5. pig
   page
   pogo
   _____

6. cling
   cage
   cart
   _____

7. lucky
   luggage
   leg
   _____

8. badge
   bag
   bad
   _____

9. cutting
   carving
   cabbage
   _____

10. fry
    fudge
    fad
    _____

11. dodge
    dog
    did
    _____

12. voting
    violin
    village
    _____

Final Hard and Soft *g*

Phonics Practice Book

Harcourt Brace School Publishers

Look at the picture. Then follow the directions.

1. Write *Pets to Go* on the sign.

2. Draw two goldfish in the aquarium.

3. Draw a cage around the bird.

4. Add a name badge to the sales clerk's shirt.

5. Draw a gate on the gerbils' pen.

6. Circle the picture of the goat.

7. Draw a hat on the goose.

8. Mark an X on the animal that does not belong in a pet store.

Now circle each soft *g* word and underline each hard *g* word in the directions.

Name _____

Find the words that fit the clues. Write the words in the puzzle.

giggle	center	citrus	cage	gas	giraffe
page	giant	fence	edge	goat	icy	go

ACROSS

1. The middle part
2. Laugh
6. Huge
7. A part of a book
9. Something that divides two back yards
10. Fuel for a car

DOWN

1. Safe home for some kinds of pets
2. An animal with a very long neck
3. The rim
4. An animal with a beard
5. A kind of fruit
8. Frozen
10. The opposite of *stop*

Review of Hard and Soft *c* and Hard and Soft *g*

Phonics Practice Book

Harcourt Brace School Publishers

Circle the word that answers each riddle. Then write the word.

1. We are tiny rodents that scurry and squeak. We are _____.

   make   mice   mug

2. I do not like to brag, but I am very, very smart. I am a _____.

   genius   canes   gentle

3. I am a bed, but I do not have pillows or blankets. I am a home for

   flowers. I am a _____.

   carton   gerbil   garden

4. I am not a boy. I am a _____.

   grill   curl   girl

5. I say "honk, honk," but I do not have a horn. I am a _____.

   goose   cost   gas

6. I am shaped like a star. A sheriff may wear me. I am a _____.

   back   badge   beg

7. I seem very big to you. To me, you look small. I am a _____.

   game   giant   icing

8. I work in a courtroom. I decide who is right and who is wrong.

   I am a _____.

   jug   goat   judge

9. I am a small wooden bird. I live in a clock. I am a _____.

   pogo   cuckoo   kicker

10. My name sounds like a country for automobiles. But I am really a flower.

    I am a _____.

    garden   certain   carnation

Name _____

Circle the word that names the picture.

1. foot / food / flute

2. slim / swim / same

3. digging / wagon / dragon

4. cloud / could / cold

5. tree / tee / tear

6. soup / scoop / coop

7. late / slate / plate

8. rise / prize / freeze

9. neck / snake / soak

Write one of the words that you circled above to complete each sentence. You will not use all of the words.

10. Would you like a _____ of ice cream?

11. A _____ is found only in fairy tales.

12. The _____ curled up on a rock in the sun.

13. Terry's goat won first _____ at the fair.

14. Will Trina play a song on her _____?

15. There was not one _____ in the blue sky.

Cumulative Review: Consonant Clusters, Hard and Soft *c* and *g*   Phonics Practice Book

Harcourt Brace School Publishers

Name_____

Write each word under the correct heading.

adult   cow   girl   skunk   twins   camp   crab
giraffe   squid   village   child   fly   judge
street   wasp   city   garden   pond   student

People	Places	Animals
_____	_____	_____
_____	_____	_____
_____	_____	_____
_____	_____	_____
_____	_____	_____
_____	_____	_____
_____	_____	_____

Fill in the circle next to the letters that complete each picture name. Then write the letters.

1
- ○ gr
- ○ sm
- ○ sn

____oke

2
- ○ sk
- ○ nd
- ○ ft

gi____

3
- ○ fr
- ○ tr
- ○ tw

____uit

4
- ○ sk
- ○ scr
- ○ squ

____are

5
- ○ bl
- ○ cl
- ○ dr

____ock

6
- ○ lt
- ○ mp
- ○ sp

sta____

7
- ○ fl
- ○ fr
- ○ bl

____y

8
- ○ sn
- ○ sk
- ○ spr

____unk

9
- ○ bl
- ○ gr
- ○ tr

____uck

10
- ○ sc
- ○ cl
- ○ cr

____ib

11
- ○ mp
- ○ nt
- ○ lk

ce____

12
- ○ st
- ○ sn
- ○ squ

____ar

13
- ○ sp
- ○ pr
- ○ fl

___etzel

14
- ○ lt
- ○ ft
- ○ nd

sa____

15
- ○ sw
- ○ str
- ○ tw

____ins

Test: Consonant Clusters, Hard and Soft *c* and *g*

Phonics Practice Book

Fill in the circle next to the sentence that tells about the picture.

1	
	◯ I love my home in the city.
	◯ It is good to live in a cave.
	◯ A tree house makes a good home.

2	
	◯ My suitcase is too big to lift now.
	◯ I like to ride my bike.
	◯ I am going on a trip to the country.

3	
	◯ A ride on my bike is great.
	◯ A hike in the forest is fun.
	◯ A walk down the street is exciting.

4	
	◯ I think I see a lion.
	◯ I think I spot an elk.
	◯ I think I see a cat.

5	
	◯ Birds swoop through the branches.
	◯ Twelve bears march past the trees.
	◯ A little skunk hides in the brush.

6	
	◯ A monkey swings on the vines.
	◯ A woodpecker drums on a tree trunk.
	◯ A crow sits on a nest.

7	
	◯ The wind makes waves on the sea.
	◯ Cars drive down the road.
	◯ The stream runs over the rocks.

8	
	◯ The lawn is brown and dry.
	◯ Grasshoppers cover the path.
	◯ Wildflowers grow on the lawn.

Name _____

church

Choose the word that names the picture. Write the word on the line. You will not use all of the words.

chimney   chat   chick   cherry   chair
carry   cheese   chain

1. _____
2. _____
3. _____
4. _____
5. _____
6. _____

Complete each sentence by writing a *ch* word from the boxes above.

7. In winter, I like to sit in my _____ by the fire.

8. Mom closes the door and locks it with the _____.

9. It is nice to see the smoke go up the _____.

10. Dad grills a _____ sandwich on the stove.

11. Then I have a dish of fruit with a _____ on top.

12. I feel as snug as a _____ inside its nest.

Digraph: Initial /ch/*ch*

Phonics Practice Book

Name _____

Write the word that names each picture.
You will not use all of the words.

patch	hatch	brush	punch	sandwich
torch	inch	pitch	peach	catch
watch	branch	stitch	church	itch

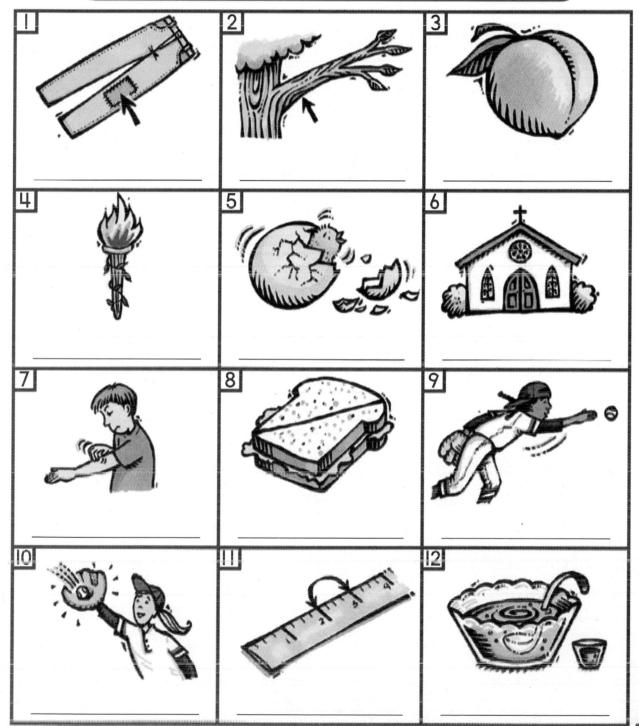

1. _____

2. _____

3. _____

4. _____

5. _____

6. _____

7. _____

8. _____

9. _____

10. _____

11. _____

12. _____

Name _____

brush

Write the word from the box that answers each clue.

| sheep | shell | cash | shop | shrimp |
| dish | shut | hush | ship | shrink |

1. It begins like *shark* and rhymes with *deep*. It is a kind of animal.

   What is it? _____

2. It begins like *cab* and rhymes with *mash*. When you have it, you can save it

   or spend it. What is it? _____

3. It begins like *hum* and rhymes with *brush*. You say it to stop a noise.

   What is it? _____

4. It begins like *shrub* and rhymes with *drink*. It happens when something

   gets smaller. What is it? _____

5. It begins like *shark* and rhymes with *stop*. You do it in a store.

   What is it? _____

6. It begins like *shark* and rhymes with *well*. You might find one by the sea.

   What is it? _____

7. It begins like *shark* and ends like *zip*. It is something that floats in the sea.

   What is it? _____

8. It begins like *did* and rhymes with *fish*. It is another word for *plate*.

   What is it? _____

9. It begins like *shark* and rhymes with *cut*. You do it to a door to close it.

   What is it? _____

10. It begins like *shrub* and rhymes with *blimp*. It is a small sea animal.

    What is it? _____

Digraphs: Initial and Final /sh/*sh*; Initial /shr/*shr*   Phonics Practice Book

Name _____

Choose the word that fits each clue. Write the words in the puzzle.

> rush   shrink   brush   shore   sheep
>
> fish   shark   shake   shrub   shorts

ACROSS

1. A large sea animal with big, sharp teeth

4. The part of the land that is next to the sea

6. Something you need to paint a picture

8. How you move your head to show "no"

9. A white, fluffy animal that lives on a farm

DOWN

1. Another word for *bush*

2. Something you may wear outdoors on a warm day

3. What some things do when they get wet

5. An animal you can catch with a worm and a hook

7. How you move when you are in a hurry

Harcourt Brace School Publishers

Name _____

 thumb   tooth   three

Write the word that names each picture. You will not use all of the words.

thermos   path   three   throne   thorn   thirteen   moth   mouth
bath   tooth   thimble   throat   think   thief   thread   thirty

1  _____	2  _____	3  _____
4  _____	5  _____	6  _____
7  _____	8  _____	9  _____
10  _____	11  _____	12  _____
13 _____	14  _____	15  _____

Digraphs: Initial and Final /th/ *th*; Initial /thr/ *thr*   Phonics Practice Book

Name _____

Dear Diary,

Guess what I did last Thursday? I went on my first roller-coaster ride! I got in line three times. Each time I got out of line to think it over. I was scared to death. The fourth time I stayed in line. My heart was thumping.

I hung on tight as the cart went up the hill. "This is a stupid thing to do," I thought. The ride up the first hill lasted about thirteen seconds. My teeth began to chatter. My head started to throb, and my heart started to thump. We went over the big hill.

The drop down took my breath away. Then I saw that the ride was smooth. It was the biggest thrill of my life. The seat felt like a throne. "This is fun!" I yelled. Now I cannot wait to go again. I could ride a thousand more times.

And that is the truth!

1. Michael rode the roller coaster last _____.

2. He was scared to _____.

3. He felt like a king on a _____.

4. The ride was fast but _____.

5. Now he wants to go back a _____ times.

Name _____

whale

Say each picture name. Write *wh* if the picture name begins with the sound you hear at the beginning of *whale*.

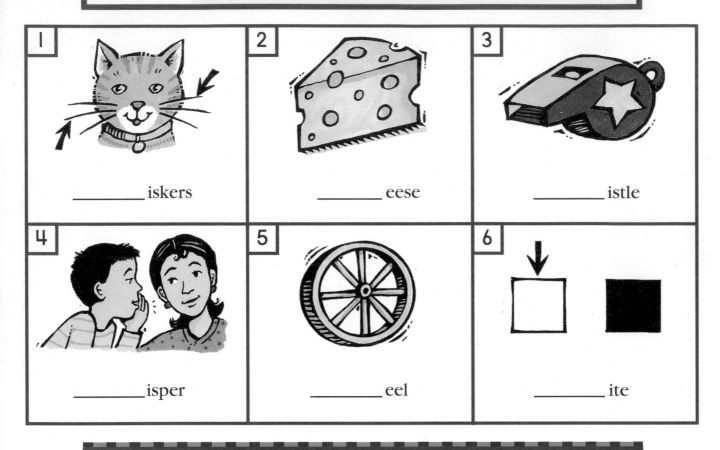

1. _____ iskers

2. _____ eese

3. _____ istle

4. _____ isper

5. _____ eel

6. _____ ite

Choose the word that completes each sentence. Write the word on the line.

wheat   when   what   why   where

7. _____ time do you wake up in the morning?

8. I wake up _____ my alarm goes off.

9. I know _____ I have to get up early.

10. I have to catch the school bus. The bus driver knows _____ I live.

11. Mom packs me a cheese sandwich on whole _____ bread for my lunch.

The words below are hidden in the puzzle. Some words go across. Some words go down. Find and circle each one.

wheat   whistle   whale   wheel   whiskers   whisper

W	H	E	E	L	Z	W	L	R	F	U	W
H	W	H	A	L	E	T	S	L	N	A	H
E	B	G	W	H	I	S	K	E	R	S	I
A	C	W	H	I	S	P	E	R	J	Y	S
T	V	J	I	R	L	X	I	Z	D	V	T
M	K	M	X	U	I	T	B	L	E	Q	L
A	D	R	E	B	X	I	S	K	G	L	E

Write the word from the puzzle that names each picture.

1. _____

2. _____

3. _____

4. _____

5. _____

6. _____

Name _____

Say each picture name. Write the letters that complete each word.

1. _____ ee	2. _____ umb	3. _____ ip	4. _____ eel
5. _____ ain	6. _____ orn	7. _____ one	8. fi _____
9. _____ ale	10. _____ imp	11. _____ air	12. _____ ow
13. _____ eep	14. tee _____	15. ben _____	16. _____ istle

Review of Digraphs: Initial and Final /ch/*ch*, /sh/*sh*, /th/*th*;
Final /ch/*tch*. Initial /shr/*shr*, /thr/*thr*, /hw/*wh*

Phonics Practice Book

Follow the directions.

1. Circle the chick that is beginning to hatch.

2. Draw a watch on the farmer's arm.

3. Draw a ribbon around the white sheep's neck.

4. Draw three apples on the branch of the tree.

5. Draw a shrub by the side of the door.

6. Circle the sack that has too much grain.

7. Write Cheep! Cheep! over the chicks.

8. Draw a thundercloud up in the sky.

9. Circle the rooster on the roof of the barn.

10. Mark an X on the brush in the farmer's hand.

11. Draw footprints on the path that leads to the barn door.

12. Draw a wreath over the horse's door.

phone

graph

Choose the word that answers each riddle.
Write the word on the line.

1. I start out in a camera. I end up in an album. I am a

   _____.

   photo   pay   phrase

2. I am a chart that shows numbers. I may have lines or bars. I am a

   _____.

   graph   great   grill

3. I am more than a word. I am less than a sentence. I am a

   _____.

   phrase   phone   prize

4. I am a name written down. If you meet a sports star, you might

   ask for one. I am an _____.

          enough   autograph   around

5. I am a large bird. I have a long, pretty tail. I am a

   _____.

   peanut   pheasant   photo

6. I am something you talk into. I am a _____.

                   phone   picnic   pink

7. I am a group of sentences. I am a _____.

                   graph   paragraph   pillow

8. I am a store where people can buy medicine. I am a

   _____.

   pharmacy   farm   phone

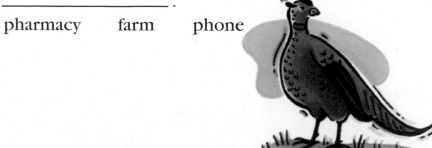

Digraph: Initial and Final /f/ph

Phonics Practice Book

Name _____

laugh

Listen to the sound the letters *gh* stand for in *laugh*.
Fill in the circle next to the sentence that tells about
the picture.

1	○ We have enough to eat.
	○ I like to look at photographs.
	○ We will eat indoors.
2	○ The ground feels rough.
	○ The dogs sleep on the mat.
	○ The pup thinks he is tough.
3	○ It is fun to read in bed.
	○ Jeff has a cold and a cough.
	○ Jeff likes to laugh.
4	○ The bird is in the tree.
	○ The monkey makes us laugh.
	○ I took a photo of the tiger.
5	○ I like to swim in the sea.
	○ Fran calls me on the phone.
	○ The rough waves rock the boat.
6	○ The pig eats under the tree.
	○ The farmer is on the phone.
	○ The horse drinks from the trough.

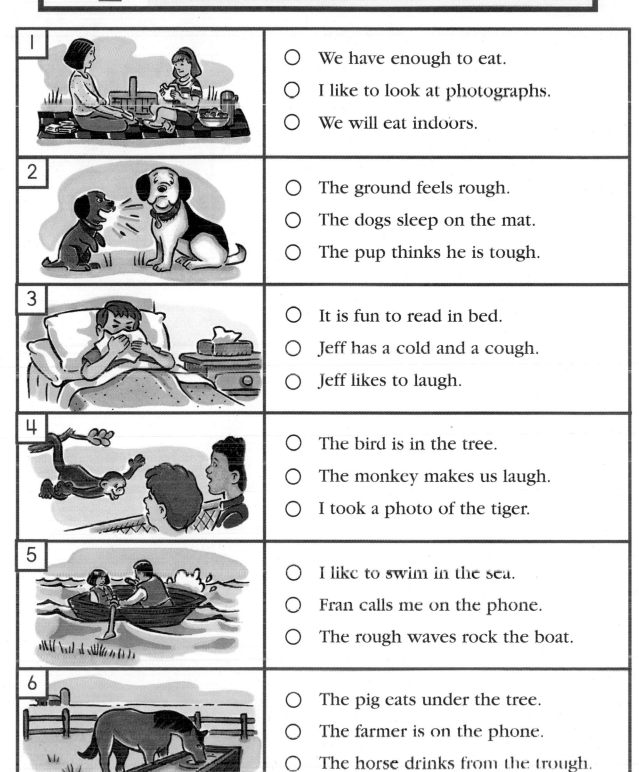

Harcourt Brace School Publishers

Digraph: Final /f/gh   231

Name _____

Listen to the sound the letters *wr* stand for in *write*. Circle the word that names the picture. Then write the word.

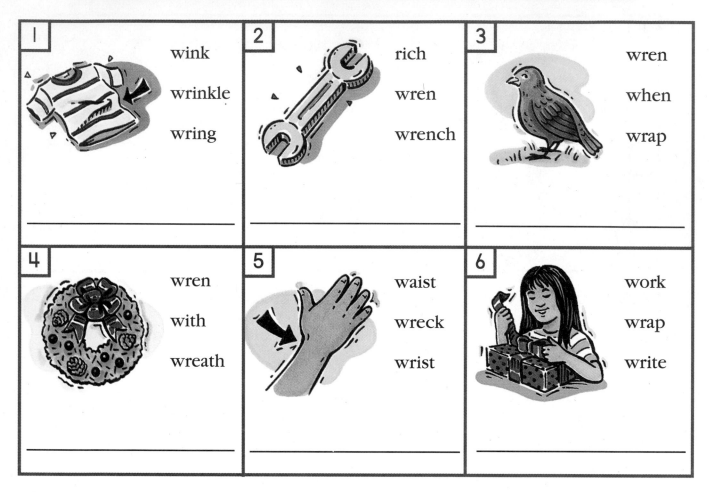

1.
wink
wrinkle
wring

_____

2.
rich
wren
wrench

_____

3.
wren
when
wrap

_____

4.
wren
with
wreath

_____

5.
waist
wreck
wrist

_____

6.
work
wrap
write

_____

Choose the correct word that answers each clue. Write the word on the line.

7. It means "not right." _____

    rang   wing   wrong

8. You do this with a pencil or pen. _____

    write   wait   read

9. You will find it around a stick of gum or a candy bar. _____

    rider   wrapper   wiper

Digraph: Initial /r/wr

Phonics Practice Book

Name _____

knight

gnat

Listen to the sound the letters *kn* and *gn* stand for in <u>kn</u>ight and <u>gn</u>at. Complete each sentence.

1. I heard a loud _____ on the door.

cook
knock
night

2. The _____ turned slowly.

not
cob
knob

3. A little green _____ stood in the doorway.

gnome
gum
name

4. He only came up to my _____.

new
key
knee

5. Please give me a bone to _____ on," he said.

grow
gnaw
gown

6. "I _____ you can find one for me," he said.

know
cow
nail

7. "If you do, I will _____ you a cap."

knit
kit
nice

8. As he rode away on a giant _____, I woke up.

go
gnat
knot

9. Then I _____ it was only a dream.

not
kit
knew

10. But how did this little cap get in my _____?

knapsack
napkin
kickoff

Name _____

skunk

ring

Listen to the sounds the letters *ng* and *nk* stand for in *ring* and *skunk*.
Read the story and answer the questions.

Eek! A Skunk!

"What are these footprints by the tree trunk?" asked Hank. "Do they belong to a chipmunk?"

"Oh, no!" said Mai Ling. "I hope I am wrong, but I think they belong to a skunk. Look! The prints lead under the porch."

"Here is a hole in the plank," said Hank. "That is its door. We can fix the hole. That will get rid of the skunk."

"Think, Hank!" groaned Mai Ling. "We might fix the hole with the skunk inside. Then the skunk will be angry. It will use its strong smell."

"I know how we can tell," said Hank. "Bring me some flour. We will sprinkle it around the porch. The skunk will walk in the flour. The prints will show where it goes. When the skunk goes out, we can fix the hole."

"Good idea!" said Mai Ling. "Let's do it right now."

1. Why did Hank and Mai Ling think that the skunk was bad news?

   _____

2. What can make a skunk use its strong smell?

   _____

3. What did Hank want to use to track the skunk?

   _____

Digraphs: Final /ng/*ng*, Final /ngk/*nk* • Reading Words in Context   Phonics Practice Book

The words below are hidden in the puzzle. Some words go across. Some words go down. Find and circle each one.

bank   bunk   rink   skunk   king
spring   wing   string   sink   trunk

S	T	R	I	N	G	B	B
I	R	I	N	K	W	U	A
N	U	K	Z	Y	I	N	N
K	N	S	K	U	N	K	K
U	K	K	I	N	G	G	Z
G	X	S	P	R	I	N	G

Write the word from the puzzle that names each picture.

1	2	3	4	5

6	7	8	9	10

Circle the word that names the picture. Then write the word.

1	rough bath laugh	2	wrench ring wren	3	knit need knee
4	gnat nap gnaw	5	sing sink sun	6	gray gift graph
7	with wreath read	8	spin spark spring	9	phone fun fine
10	stung shack skunk	11	gnome note game	12	kick king cane
13	photo foot pot	14	nice kite knight	15	rink ring rich

Review of Digraphs: /f/*ph, gh*; /r/*wr*; /n/*kn, gn*;
Final /ng/*ng*, /ngk/*nk*

Phonics Practice Book

Harcourt Brace School Publishers

Follow the directions.

1. Write your name on the sign over the door.

2. Circle the words that begin with the same sound as *rink*.

3. Write "THANK YOU" on the sign on the doorknob.

4. Draw a bow on the wreath.

5. Draw a patch on the knee of the worker's pants.

6. Circle the wrench.

7. Draw an arrow that points to the worker's right wrist.

8. Write *Ring!* next to the phone.

9. Add something to the picture that makes you laugh.

CHECK-UP

Fill in the circle next to the word that names the picture.

1

- ○ chair
- ○ store
- ○ shark

_____

2
- ○ watch
- ○ what
- ○ rich

_____

3
- ○ gruff
- ○ graph
- ○ gray

_____

4
- ○ sink
- ○ skunk
- ○ stuck

_____

5
- ○ bank
- ○ branch
- ○ brace

_____

6
- ○ scrub
- ○ skip
- ○ shrub

_____

7
- ○ desk
- ○ dust
- ○ dish

_____

8
- ○ laugh
- ○ tough
- ○ lift

_____

9
- ○ wings
- ○ swing
- ○ snug

_____

10
- ○ fin
- ○ phone
- ○ fan

_____

11
- ○ thread
- ○ think
- ○ talk

_____

12
- ○ cup
- ○ champ
- ○ chick

_____

13
- ○ wren
- ○ rip
- ○ when

_____

14
- ○ gnome
- ○ grew
- ○ know

_____

15
- ○ keep
- ○ need
- ○ knee

_____

Harcourt Brace School Publishers

Name _____

Read the story and find out what happens when Sharman meets a whale.

A WHALE OF A WISH

Sharman loved to watch the sea. One day she saw something big floating near the shore. Sharman could not believe her eyes. It was a whale!

"What are you doing here?" Sharman asked. "Do you know that you are in very shallow water?"

"I am lost," groaned the whale. "If you help me get back to the deep sea, I will grant you a wish."

"Just swing around and follow the sun," said Sharman. "You will be in the deep sea very soon."

"Thank you," said the whale. "Now what is your wish?"

"I'll just wish you home safely," said Sharman. So, with a swish of its tail, the whale swam out to sea.

Fill in the circle next to the correct answer.

1. What did Sharman see floating near the shore?
   ○ some shells
   ○ a whale
   ○ some cheers

2. What was the whale's problem?
   ○ The water was too shallow.
   ○ He was near a shark.
   ○ He was sinking.

3. How did Sharman help the whale?
   ○ She swished his tail.
   ○ She gave him a wish.
   ○ She told him how to find the deep sea.

Harcourt Brace School Publishers

A shorter way to write *he is* is *he's*. *He's* is a contraction. To make a contraction, use an apostrophe (') in place of one or more letters that are left out. In contractions, *am, not, will,* and *is* can be shortened to *'m, n't, 'll,* and *'s*.

I am = I'm   can not = can't   she will = she'll

Combine the word at the top of each box with the words below it to write contractions. Be sure to use an (') to show letters that are left out.

not		**will**	
1. could	_____	6. he	_____
2. does	_____	7. she	_____
3. can	_____	8. I	_____
4. were	_____	9. you	_____
5. do	_____		

am

10. I _____

is

11. he _____   12. she _____   13. it _____

Contractions: *'m, n't, 'll, 's*   Phonics Practice Book

Name _____

In contractions, *had* and *would* can be shortened to *'d*.
Have and *are* can be shortened to *'ve* and *'re*.

we had = we'd   you have = you've
you would = you'd   they are = they're

Write the two words that make each contraction. Then write the letters that were left out.

Contraction	two words	letters left out
1. I've	_____	_____
2. he'd	_____	_____
3. we're	_____	_____
4. she'd	_____	_____

Write the contraction that can be made by combining the two underlined words. Remember to use an apostrophe (') to show letters that are left out.

5. "You would make a great shortstop," my coach said. _____

6. "I have been thinking about trying that," I said. _____

7. "They have got a good shortstop on the other team," said Coach.

_____

8. "So, we had better let you practice," he said. _____

For each sentence, form a contraction from the words in parentheses ( ). Write the contraction.

New School Rules

1. (I am) (we will) _____ about to tell you a couple of new

   rules that _____ all need to follow at school.

2. (should not) You _____ fly an airplane through the door.

3. (cannot) At lunch, your snake _____ ask for more.

4. (we are) (it is) When _____ on a field trip,

   _____ nice to wear your best.

5. (would not) Of course you _____ come in a wedding

   dress.

6. (You have) _____ turned in your homework every day,

   I think.

7. (you would) (were not) But _____ get a much better

   grade if it _____ in invisible ink!

8. (do not) (it will) If you _____ forget these simple rules,

   _____ make for a much happier school.

Harcourt Brace School Publishers

Harcourt Brace School Publishers

Do you think you'd be surprised at what a magnet can pick up? If you've tried it, you'll know that magnets won't pick up anything that isn't made of a certain material. Do you know what that material is? If you don't, you're about to find out!

A magnet doesn't pick up a piece of paper. It's not going to pick up a pencil, either. What are these two things made from? They're made from wood, of course. What about plastic toys—will a magnet pick them up? No, it won't. What about rocks or glass? A magnet can't move them at all. Could a magnet pick up a metal paper clip? If it couldn't, then it isn't a magnet! Magnets pick up only things that have iron in them. You'll have to test this for yourself some time.

1. Write a title for the selection that uses a contraction.

_____

2. What are some things that a magnet can't pick up?

_____

Name _____

Chad's bike

An apostrophe and *s* (*'s*) at the end of a word can show that one person or animal owns something. Read each phrase. If it contains a word that shows someone owns something, write the word. The first one has been done for you.

1. Ahmed's toy _____Ahmed's_____

2. Grandma's bag _____

3. flowers growing _____

4. rows of boxes _____

5. cats sleep _____

6. Elena's shorts _____

Change the underlined words in each phrase to one word with *'s*.

7. the desk <u>that belongs to my brother</u>

   my _____ desk

8. the necklace <u>that belongs to Mom</u>

   _____ necklace

9. the hat <u>that belongs to the firefighter</u>

   the _____ hat

10. The skates <u>that belong to Connie</u>

    _____ skates

Possessive: *'s*

Phonics Practice Book

Harcourt Brace School Publishers

An *s* and an apostrophe (*s'*) at the end of a word can show that more than one person or animal owns something.

Read the first sentence in each pair. In the second sentence, write the underlined word in a way that shows that more than one person or animal owns or has something.

my parents' car

1. We saw several <u>puppies</u> at the shelter.

   The _____ coats had black spots.

2. Ken picked up the toys belonging to the <u>kittens</u>.

   Now the _____ toys are put away.

3. The bikes that belong to the <u>girls</u> are in the driveway.

   We need to move the _____ bikes.

4. Our <u>friends</u> ordered a cheese pizza.

   We will share our _____ pizza.

5. The crops of the <u>farmers</u> are good this year.

   The fruit stand is full of the _____ crops.

6. The <u>boys</u> were out on the beach too long.

   Now the _____ faces are red.

7. Boxes of new books came in for the <u>teachers</u>.

   The _____ books are in the classroom.

8. Mr. Moon took photos of all of the <u>classes</u>.

   The _____ photos turned out well.

Harcourt Brace School Publishers

REVIEW Read the book titles. Write words from the titles in the correct places on the chart.

<table>
<tr><td colspan="2" align="center">**Words That Show
One Owner**</td><td colspan="2" align="center">**Words That Show
More Than One Owner**</td></tr>
</table>

_____	_____
_____	_____
_____	_____
_____	_____
_____	_____
_____	_____
_____	_____

Harcourt Brace School Publishers

Name _____

Look at the number of animals in each picture. Label each home to show whether it belongs to one animal or more than one animal.

1 bear

the _____ cave

2 parrot

the _____ perch

3 goat

the _____ mountain

4 seal

the _____ pond

5 lizard

the _____ garden

6 crocodile

the _____ river

7 monkey

the _____ trees

8 fish

the _____ pond

9 prairie dog

the _____ burrow

10 turtle

the _____ beach

11 snake

the _____ tank

12 lion

the _____ den

Write the two words that each contraction stands for.

1. shouldn't   _____   _____

2. haven't   _____   _____

3. it's   _____   _____

4. you'd   _____   _____

5. they're   _____   _____

6. I'm   _____   _____

7. we'll   _____   _____

8. you're   _____   _____

9. I've   _____   _____

10. he'd   _____   _____

11. she's   _____   _____

12. they'll   _____   _____

13. couldn't   _____   _____

14. they'd   _____   _____

Harcourt Brace School Publishers

Name _____

Change the underlined words in each phrase to a word with 's or s'.

1. the watch <u>that belongs to Ann</u> _____ watch

2. the shirt <u>that belongs to Adam</u> _____ shirt

3. the bikes <u>that belong to the boys</u> the _____ bikes

4. the houses <u>that belong to the dogs</u> the _____ houses

5. the letter <u>that belongs to Amy</u> _____ letter

6. the suitcase <u>that belongs to our friends</u> our _____ suitcase

7. the song <u>that Grandpa wrote</u> _____ song

8. the shadow <u>made by Rico</u> _____ shadow

9. the hot dog <u>that belongs to Mrs. French</u> _____ hot dog

10. the feathers <u>that the ducks have</u> the_____ feathers

11. the sounds <u>of the horns</u> the _____ sounds

12. the screens <u>that go with the computers</u> the_____ screens

13. the keys <u>that belong to the teacher</u> the _____ keys

14. the wings <u>that the butterflies have</u> the _____ wings

15. the cake <u>for the twins</u> the _____ cake

Harcourt Brace School Publishers

Complete each sentence by adding *s, es, ed,* or *ing* to the word in front of the sentence

Today
I jump.
The frog jump<u>s</u> too.
The frog and I are jump<u>ing</u>.
My dad watch<u>es</u> us.
Yesterday
The frog jump<u>ed</u>, and I did not.

1. play   The Lan family enjoys _____ music every day.

2. start   The children _____ playing when they

    were very young.

3. sing   Mei Ling _____ and plays the flute.

4. want   Tran plays the violin, but last year he _____

    to learn to play the harp.

5. wish   He _____ he could play both.

6. listen   Mrs. Lan smiles as she _____ to her

    children play.

7. talk   Last week, they _____ about

    giving a concert.

8. look   They are _____ for

    a place to hold a concert.

9. ask   Last Tuesday, the Lans _____ me to help them find

    a place.

10. wait   The Lans are just _____ for the special day when

    they can give the concert.

Inflected Endings: -s, -es, -ed, -ing

Phonics Practice Book

Name _____

	Base Word	Base Word + s or es	Base Word + ed	Base Word + ing
1	discuss	_____	_____	_____
2	_____	thanks	_____	_____
3	_____	_____	talked	_____
4	_____	works	_____	_____
5	_____	_____	_____	cleaning

Use a word from the chart to complete each sentence.

6. Last month we _____ our trip to visit a city worker.

7. Today we arrived at the park, and the city worker _____
   to our class.

8. He _____ hard to keep parks and streams clean.

9. We say we will help, and now we are _____ up a stream.

10. The city worker _____ us for helping him.

Harcourt Brace School Publishers

In most short-vowel words that end with one consonant, double the final consonant before adding *ed* or *ing*.

Today	Yesterday
Pam and I jog.	Yesterday, it rained
Sam is jog<u>ging</u> too.	while Pam jog<u>ged</u>.

Double the final consonant before adding *ed* and *ing* to each base word. Write the words.

1	clap	2	put	3	grab
	_____		_____		_____
	_____		_____		_____
4	stop	5	plan	6	run
	_____		_____		_____
	_____		_____		_____

Use a word from above to complete each sentence. You will not use all of the words.

7. Yesterday we _____ to go for a swim when my cousin arrived.

8. Today my cousin is here, and we are _____ to the lake.

9. Now we are _____ on our swim fins.

10. When we get out of the water, we will _____ our towels.

Inflected Endings: *-ed, -ing*

Phonics Practice Book

Harcourt Brace School Publishers

Name _____

What Pat Did Yesterday

mop   jog   clap

_____

_____

_____

What Pat Is Doing Today

swim   chat   dig

_____

_____

_____

Add *ed* or *ing* to the underlined word to complete the second sentence in each pair.

1. My mom and I <u>plant</u> flowers in the garden.

   We are _____ two different kinds of flowers.

2. Mom and I each <u>dig</u> a hole in the ground.

   I am _____ a deeper hole than Mom's.

3. I <u>put</u> a pretty daisy in the hole.

   Mom is _____ in an orange geranium.

4. I <u>pat</u> the soil around my flower.

   Mom is _____ the soil around her flower more firmly than I am.

5. Now we <u>pour</u> water on our flowers.

   The last time we planted flowers, I _____ too much water on mine.

Name _____

Read the paragraphs, and think about what they tell you.

An Eclipse of the Sun

Have you ever seen an eclipse of the sun? Bet you were wondering what was happening. If so, you saw the sky get dark in the middle of the day.

People long ago were afraid when there was an eclipse. They would start running and screaming. But we know now that an eclipse is nothing to be afraid of.

An eclipse happens when the moon passes in a straight line between the earth and the sun. For a short time, the moon blocks the light of the sun. Then the moon passes out of the way, and sunlight once again touches the earth.

Write the answers to the questions.

1. What happens to the sky during an eclipse of the sun?

   _____

2. What brings about an eclipse of the sun?

   _____

3. How does an eclipse of the sun end?

   _____

4. Long ago, what did people do when they saw an eclipse?

   _____

Review of Inflected Endings: -s, -es, -ed, -ing

Phonics Practice Book

Harcourt Brace School Publishers

Name _____

Add the correct ending to the underlined base word in each sentence. Write the new words in the puzzle.

Across

1. My canary <u>sing</u> as I eat my breakfast.
3. The girl is <u>bring</u> some food for her pet.
5. My cat <u>rub</u> against my legs last night.
7. The rabbit <u>munch</u> on the carrots I give it.
9. My cat <u>purr</u> when I stroked her fur yesterday.
11. The boy <u>hunt</u> for his lost book last week.
13. I am <u>run</u> in a race today.

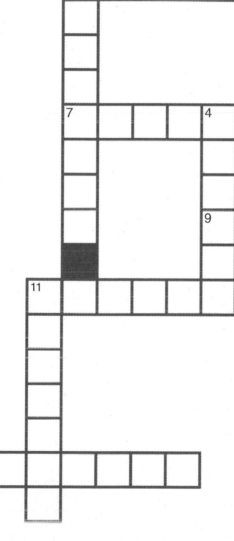

Down

1. The fish are <u>swim</u> in the tank.
2. We are <u>pat</u> soil around the new plants.
3. The dog <u>bark</u> as a stranger passes by.
4. The frog <u>hop</u> onto the lily pad just a minute ago.
11. That girl is <u>hum</u> while she walks to school.

Name _____

In words that end with silent *e*, drop the *e* before adding *ed* or *ing*. Drop the silent *e* and add *ed* and *ing* to each base word. Write the new words.

Dad and I bake cakes and pies.

Dad bak<u>ed</u> a cake yesterday.

Dad is bak<u>ing</u> a pie today.

1 save	2 slice
_____ _____	_____ _____
3 rake	4 tape
_____ _____	_____ _____
5 name	6 dance
_____ _____	_____ _____
7 race	8 paste
_____ _____	_____ _____

Inflected Endings: *-ed, -ing*

Read the story and answer the questions.

Today I am writing about my trip to my grandma's house. Last Saturday, my friend Trina and I went to my grandma's house in the country. Grandma brought us a picnic lunch and we walked down to the stream.

After we ate, we waded in the water. For a while, we bounced rocks across the stream. Trina got bored, so we raced back to the house. Grandma had a surprise. She had just baked a peach pie! She gave us some with ice cream.

When it was time to leave, Trina told Grandma and me she had had a great day. She said she could not remember ever having so much fun. I loved it, too. I always enjoy going to Grandma's house.

1. Name three things the girls did at Grandma's house.

_____

_____

2. How does the girl feel about going to her grandma's house? How do you know?

_____

3. What was Grandma's surprise?

_____

Harcourt Brace School Publishers

Name _____

In a word that ends in *f* or *fe*, change the *f* or *fe* to *v* and add *es* to make it mean more than one. Add *es* to each word. Write the new word.

one wo<u>lf</u>   two wo<u>lves</u>   one kni<u>fe</u>   two kni<u>ves</u>

1	knife _____	2	elf _____
3	leaf _____	4	thief _____
5	life _____	6	loaf _____
7	shelf _____	8	half _____
9	wife _____	10	calf _____

Use a word from above to complete each sentence.

11. Mom baked three _____ of bread today.

12. We ate apple _____ for a snack at school.

13. Mr. Brown let us feed the _____ on his farm.

14. Sam and Pete raked the _____ in Mrs. Smith's yard.

Inflected Ending: *-es*

Phonics Practice Book

In a base word that ends with a consonant followed by *y*, drop the *y* before adding *ies*. For each base word below, drop the final *y* and add *ies*. Write the new word.

The baby can cry. The baby cries.

1 spy	2 copy	3 fly
_____	_____	_____
4 carry	5 try	6 hurry
_____	_____	_____

Use a word from above to complete each sentence.

7. A cat _____ a butterfly resting on a flower.

8. The cat _____ to chase the butterfly.

9. The butterfly _____ away quickly.

10. The cat _____ after it, but still it cannot

catch the beautiful butterfly.

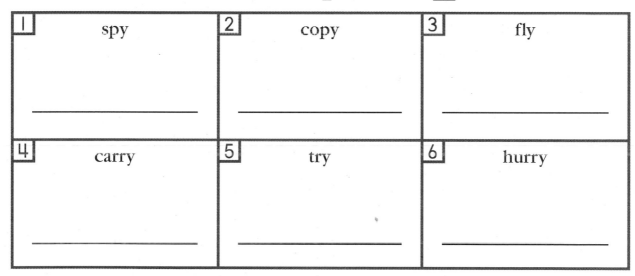

Read the story and answer the questions.

My aunt works in a diner. She likes her job. I like to go to see her there. The food is good, and the people are friendly. The diner is busy.

My aunt takes people's orders and carries out the food on a big tray. She rushes around and hurries to get people the things they ask for. She says she always tries to be friendly and nice to people.

After the diner is closed, my aunt dries the dishes. Sometimes I help, too. When we get home, she empties her pockets, and I count her tips. She studies the newspaper. Sometimes she spies on me to make sure I am counting the money right!

1. Why does the boy like the diner?

   _____

2. Name four things the boy's aunt does at her job in the diner.

   _____

   _____

3. What would be a good title for this story?

   _____

Harcourt Brace School Publishers

Read the book titles. Then write the base word for each word in the boxes.

1	grows	2	smiling
	_____		_____
3	cries	4	scarves
	_____		_____
5	stopped	6	loved
	_____		_____
7	giving	8	sleeps
	_____		_____
9	bringing	10	scared
	_____		_____

Harcourt Brace School Publishers

SUPER REVIEW

Write the base word for the underlined word in each sentence.

1. Our dad <u>tries</u> to teach us to do things to help clean up the earth. _____

2. He <u>likes</u> for us to recycle paper and cans each week. _____

3. He also <u>wants</u> us to grow some of our own food. _____

4. My little sister and I <u>planted</u> some bean seeds in pots. _____

5. Dad said, "Put them in the window and make sure the sun is <u>shining</u> on them."

   _____

6. Every day my sister <u>rushes</u> over to look at the pots. _____

7. Earlier this morning she shouted, "They <u>sprouted</u> last night!" _____

8. My little sister <u>clapped</u> her hands when she saw the tiny plants. _____

9. I saw little green shoots <u>popping</u> up through the soil. _____

10. Soon we will be <u>eating</u> the beans that we have grown. _____

11. My dad has <u>asked</u> us to think of some other ways we can keep the earth

    clean. _____

12. He says our <u>lives</u> will be better if the earth is clean and healthy.

    _____

Harcourt Brace School Publishers

Write the base word for the underlined word in each sentence.

1. Last week we <u>planned</u> a camping trip. _____

2. Today we are <u>staying</u> in a tent at our beautiful campsite. _____

3. The sun is <u>shining</u> brightly. _____

4. But every time we leave the campsite, a bear <u>tries</u> to get our food.

   _____

5. Mom <u>fusses</u> at us if we leave food sitting out. _____

6. We are <u>hoping</u> the bear has gotten tired of our campsite, but it hasn't.

   _____

7. It keeps <u>walking</u> up to our campsite when we are not there.

   _____

8. A little while ago, we tried to go back to the tent but we <u>stopped</u> when we saw

   the bear. _____

9. It was eating all of our <u>loaves</u> of honey bread. _____

10. Dad <u>wants</u> to scare the bear away. _____

11. We are <u>getting</u> tired of waiting. _____

12. Finally the bear <u>runs</u> away! _____

Name _____

Complete the chart by adding the ending at the top to the base word.

		s or es	ing	ed
1	start			
2	skid			
3	wish			
4	play			
5	watch			
6	clap			

Write the base word.

7	grabbed _____	8	sings _____	9	trying _____
10	dishes _____	11	leaves _____	12	stopping _____
13	spies _____	14	picked _____	15	chatting _____
16	pitches _____	17	dries _____	18	taped _____

Inflected Endings Test

Phonics Practice Book

Name _____

A prefix is added to the beginning of a base word to make a new word with a different meaning. Write the word with *un-* or *re-* that matches each meaning.

un = not
re = again

1	use again	2	not kind	3	join again
	_____		_____		_____

4	build again	5	not able	6	write again
	_____		_____		_____

7	not true	8	not happy	9	fill again
	_____		_____		_____

10	not afraid	11	tell again	12	not safe
	_____		_____		_____

Add the prefix *im-* to each word. Then write a word to complete each sentence.

im = not

13	patient	14	perfect	15	polite
	_____		_____		_____

16. My family says that being late is

_____ .

17. When we are getting ready to go somewhere, they are quite _____ with me.

18. I think that makes them _____ , too!

Harcourt Brace School Publishers

Add the prefix _im-_ or _re-_ to the underlined word to complete each sentence.

1. If water is not clean and <u>pure</u>, then it is _____.

2. If you <u>check</u> your work again, you _____ it.

3. If you <u>pay</u> back money that you owe, you _____ it.

4. If you <u>tie</u> your shoe again, you _____ it.

5. If an action is not <u>proper</u>, then it is _____.

6. If someone is not <u>mature</u>, then he or she is _____.

7. If you <u>place</u> an item back on the shelf, you _____ it.

8. If something is not <u>possible</u>, then it is _____.

9. If you <u>read</u> a book a second time, you _____ it.

10. If you turn in work that is not <u>perfect</u>, it might be called

    _____.

Add the prefix _re-_ to each base word.

11. pack   _____

12. cover   _____

13. load   _____

14. tie   _____

15. do   _____

Prefixes: _re-, im-_

Phonics Practice Book

Harcourt Brace School Publishers

Read the selection, and then answer the questions.

Bats Bats Bats

Many stories told about bats are untrue. That is why people may react badly when they see bats. Many things that bats do in stories and movies are impossible. Bats can fly like birds. But unlike birds, bats are mammals. All other mammals are unable to fly.

Many bats live in caves. If you go during the day to see bats fly out of a cave, you may become impatient. Bats sleep all day, hanging upside down. At sunset they unfold their wings. Then they fly out of the cave to rejoin the outside world.

Bats fly around looking for food. They help people by eating insects that are pests. So, the next time you see a bat, don't be afraid. If someone tells you something unlikely about bats, ask the person to recheck their facts.

1. What can be said of many of the things bats do in stories and movies?

   _____

2. Why do some people react badly when they see bats?

   _____

3. How does the selection say bats are different from birds?

   _____

4. How do bats spend their time during the day?

   _____

5. How do bats help people?

   _____

non = not or without   **pre** = before   **dis** = the opposite of
Use the prefixes *non, pre,* and *dis* to write a word to match each meaning.

1 not a believer	2 to pay before	3 the opposite of *like*
4 not making sense	5 to judge before the right time	6 the opposite of *honest*
7 not toxic	8 to plan before	9 to view before
10 without a stop	11 the opposite of *appear*	12 the opposite of *order*

Use a word you just wrote to complete each sentence. You will not use all of the words.

13. The messy room was in a state of _____.

14. Something was sure to get lost and _____.

15. We sat down to _____ who would do the job.

16. Then we worked _____ to get the work done.

Prefixes: *non-, pre-, dis-*

Phonics Practice Book

Name _____

1. If you do not <u>continue</u> to play a game, you _____ it.

2. If you are not yet a teen, you are a _____.

3. If you do not feel <u>comfort</u>, then you might feel _____.

4. The steps a pilot follows before a <u>flight</u> are called _____ checks.

5. Things that happened before <u>historic</u> times are _____.

6. A baseball team that does not have the <u>advantage</u> of having good hitters is usually at a _____.

Add the prefix _non-_ to each base word.

7. verbal

_____

9. sense

_____

8. skid

_____

10. stop

_____

Write a word you just wrote to complete each sentence.

11. Mom says that buying fancy tennis shoes is _____.

12. I think good shoes are important when you play sports _____.

13. I even told her that the _____ soles would keep me from slipping.

14. She did not say anything, but her _____ clues still told me "no."

Harcourt Brace School Publishers

Name _____

What Happened to the Dinosaurs?

Experts disagree about what happened to the creatures that predated other animals. Some scientists say that the dinosaurs disappeared because of changes in the weather. They think it became too cold for dinosaurs to live.

Other scientists say that a huge meteor crashed into the Earth. They think clouds of dust killed many kinds of plants. Many dinosaurs would have had nothing to eat.

Since there are no records of that time, it is hard to disprove one idea or the other. People may wonder for a long time what really happened to those prehistoric creatures. Until proof is found, people can study dinosaurs' nonextinct relatives—reptiles and birds.

Harcourt Brace School Publishers

1. Why could a meteor have caused dinosaurs to die out?

_____

_____

2. Why is it hard to disprove ideas about dinosaurs?

_____

3. What nonextinct relatives of dinosaurs can we study today?

_____

The words below are in the puzzle. Some words go down. Some words go across. Find and circle each one.

| prejudge | disband | improper | undo | nonstick | pretest |
| untrue | refill | nonsense | disobey | impolite | reheat |

```
i  m  p  r  o  p  e  r  b
b  d  i  s  b  a  n  d  l
z  t  v  j  i  q  a  d  m
q  j  p  r  e  t  e  s  t
i  k  n  n  j  b  k  e  n
e  p  r  x  v  q  b  k  o
l  r  e  h  e  a  t  c  n
u  e  g  u  n  d  o  b  s
t  j  h  c  b  w  m  o  t
t  u  n  t  r  u  e  k  i
i  d  i  s  o  b  e  y  c
g  g  o  p  r  i  x  t  k
r  e  f  i  l  l  n  z  u
n  o  n  s  e  n  s  e  p
r  i  m  p  o  l  i  t  e
```

Write a word you circled in the puzzle to answer each question.

1. This word means "to not obey."   _____

2. This word means "to fill again."   _____

3. This word means "to judge before."   _____

4. This word means "not true."   _____

Name _____

Dear Misha,

    Did you know that some kinds of wolves are in danger of becoming extinct? Some people in my state are trying to rebuild the wolf population in my area. It is uncertain whether they will be able to help. Some people dislike the idea of having wolves rejoin the wildlife here. They feel it will be unsafe for farm animals. But I think that's nonsense. If the wolves don't get help, it will be impossible for them to recover and live in the wild. What do you think? I'd like to hear whether you agree or disagree with me.

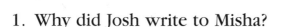

    Your pen pal,
    Josh

1. Why did Josh write to Misha?

   _____

2. Why is Josh not sure if the group will be able to help the wolves?

   _____

3. Why do some people dislike the idea of the wolves rejoining the local

   wildlife? _____

4. What does Josh think about wolves?

   _____

Harcourt Brace School Publishers

Name _____

The suffixes *-ly* and *-ful* can be added to the end of base words to change their meaning.
    -ly = in a certain way   -ful = full of or enough to fill
Add the suffix to each word below it. Write the new words.

-ly

1. slow _____
2. loud _____
3. quiet _____
4. neat _____
5. quick _____
6. poor _____

-ful

7. care _____
8. help _____
9. thought _____
10. thank _____
11. cheer _____
12. hope _____

Use some of the new words you made to complete the sentences.

13. I wanted to finish my homework _____ so I could go outside and play.

14. I wrote my spelling words _____ so that they were easy to read.

15. I had a question about my math homework, and my sister was

_____.

16. I was _____ that she could help.

17. I closed my books and _____ put my things away.

18. My sister said that I was

_____

for being so quiet.

Harcourt Brace School Publishers

Add -ly or -ful to each base word to complete each sentence.

1. care   We are always _____ when we cross the street.

2. safe   The crossing guard helps us get _____ to the other side.

3. brave   She _____ stops traffic for us.

4. near   One day there was _____ an accident.

5. foolish   A little boy _____ dashed in front of a car.

6. Fortunate   _____ ,the car was able to stop.

7. quick   If the driver had not reacted _____ , the boy could have been hurt.

8. fear   The driver was _____ that someone had been hurt.

9. thank   When she saw that no one was hurt, she looked

    _____ .

10. tear   The little boy was fine but _____ .

11. help   The crossing guard was _____ in getting the boy to calm down.

12. kind   The guard _____ explained to the boy what he should do next time.

Harcourt Brace School Publishers

Suffixes: -ly, -ful

able = able to be, able to give   less = without

Add the suffix -able or -less to write a word to match each definition.

1 able to be washed _____	**2** without joy _____	**3** able to give comfort _____
4 without sleep _____	**5** able to be noticed _____	**6** able to be remarked upon _____
7 without a care _____	**8** without thought _____	**9** able to be worked _____

Add -able or -less to the base word to complete each phrase.

10. port _____ television

11. sugar _____ gum

12. value _____ jewelry
    (hint: drop the final e)

13. seed _____ grapes

14. adore _____ teddy bear (hint: drop the final e)

15. love _____ pet (hint: drop the final e)

Name _____

Choose the word that completes each sentence. Write the words in the puzzle.

toothless   thoughtless   cloudless
washable   remarkable   tasteless
adorable   helpless   portable

ACROSS
1. Water has no taste. It is _____.
3. My radio is easy to take with me because it is _____.
5. The sky was clear and _____.
7. The baby had a _____ grin.

DOWN
1. Leaving without saying goodbye was _____.
2. I read the most _____ story.
4. I am glad my new shirt is _____.
6. I try to solve my own problems rather than be _____.
10. The new puppy was _____ .

Suffixes: -able, -less

Phonics Practice Book

Name _____

-less   -able
-ly   -ful

1. If the night sky seems to have not even one <u>star</u>, then

   it is _____ .

2. If you are moving at a <u>slow</u> speed, you are moving _____ .

3. If your jeans can be put in the <u>wash</u>, they are _____ .

4. If you have enough sugar to fill one <u>cup</u>, you have a _____ .

5. If you enjoy the <u>comfort</u> of your bed, it is a _____ place.

6. If you are full of <u>joy</u>, you are _____ .

7. If you did not <u>sleep</u> last night, you had a _____ night.

8. If you speak in a <u>loud</u> way, your family might say you

   speak _____ .

9. If you had a day full of <u>wonder</u>, you had a _____ day.

10. If you are brave and without <u>fear</u>, you are a _____ person.

11. If you can <u>train</u> your pet to do tricks, your pet is _____ .

12. If you are finishing this <u>page</u> in a <u>quick</u> way, you are

    finishing _____ .

Harcourt Brace School Publishers

Name _____

Write a word to complete each sentence.

cupful fearless careful lovely quickly sleepless
neatly remarkable moveable kindly mouthful slowly

1. Please be _____ when you hold the new puppy.

2. That animal trick was amazing and _____.

3. Please write your name _____ on the page.

4. The firefighters were brave and _____ during the blaze.

5. It is impolite to talk with a _____ of food.

6. My neighbor would like to borrow a _____ of sugar.

7. The police officer spoke _____ to the lost child.

8. This toy has a lot of _____ parts.

9. We spent a _____ night because the storm was so loud.

10. Mom said the painting I made was _____.

11. The small rabbit ran away _____ when it saw the fox.

12. I chew my food _____ so I can enjoy every bite.

Name _____

impolite   prejudge   lovable   unsafe   washable
sugarless   blameless   neatly   softly   dislike
reread   fearful   nonstop   dishonest   joyful

1. able to be washed _____

2. in a neat way _____

3. without sugar _____

4. to read again _____

5. without a stop _____

6. in a soft way _____

7. to judge before the right time _____

8. without blame _____

9. able to be loved _____

10. full of joy _____

11. not safe _____

12. opposite of honest _____

13. not polite _____

14. full of fear _____

15. the opposite of *like* _____

Write the prefix or suffix that completes each statement.

1. _____ + historic = before historic times

2. tender + _____ = in a tender way

3. _____ + pack = to pack again

4. _____ + sense = not making sense

5. _____ + agree = the opposite of *agree*

6. cup + _____ = amount to fill a cup

7. _____ + opened = not opened

8. _____ + possible = not possible

9. thought + _____ = without thought

10. train + _____ = able to be trained

11. _____ + certain = not certain

12. sleep + _____ = without sleep

13. _____ + obey = the opposite of *obey*

14. _____ + healthy = not healthy

Cumulative Review of Prefixes and Suffixes   Phonics Practice Book

Add -er and -est to each word. Write the new words in the chart.

Beth is *tall*.   **Kim is *taller* than Beth.**   **Mary is the *tallest* one.**

	Word + *-er*	Word + *-est*
1. fresh	_____	_____
2. kind	_____	_____
3. sweet	_____	_____
4. light	_____	_____
5. hard	_____	_____
6. warm	_____	_____
7. long	_____	_____
8. loud	_____	_____
9. short	_____	_____
10. clear	_____	_____

Use some of the new words you wrote to complete the sentences.

11. I like the summer when the days get longer. In fact, the

    _____ day of the year is in June.

12. In June the weather gets _____ with each day that passes.

13. I begin to wear shorts and _____ clothing to keep cool.

14. The vegetables from our garden taste _____ than the ones

    from the store.

15. Summer is when we get the _____ peaches, berries, and

    melons.

Read the first sentence in each pair. Complete the second sentence by adding *er* or *est* to the word in bold print.

1. Allen is **strong.**

   Jack is _____.

2. Ann's sweater is **warm.**

   Her mom's coat is _____.

3. All of the pencils are **short.**

   The pencil on the right is the _____.

4. The penny is **light.**

   The feather is _____.

5. The boys on the team are **tall.**

   The boy at the end of the line is the _____.

6. The rope is **strong.**

   The chain is even _____.

7. Michael wore a **dark** cap to the game.

   His dad wore a _____ one.

Comparatives and Superlatives: -er, -est

Phonics Practice Book

Look at the picture, and follow the directions.

This is the

_____

comfortable chair
of all.

1. Write *We Have the Most Affordable Prices in Town* on the wall.

2. Circle the table that is more expensive than the yellow table.

3. Complete the girl's thought.

4. Draw flowers in the vase to make the room look more beautiful.

5. Draw two pillows on the most expensive couch.

6. Put an X on the more slender lamp.

7. Complete these sentences with *more* or *most*.

• The red couch is _____ expensive than the brown one.

• The white couch is the _____ expensive one of all.

Harcourt Brace School Publishers

Name _____

My sister is intelligent—
Awards hang on her wall.
But even more intelligent
Is my big brother, Paul.

I'm good at math and science.
A whiz at basketball.
It's clear to me that I'm the most
Intelligent of all.

My mom says, "Be more modest,
Like Sis and brother Paul."
I'm modest—clearly, I am the
Most modest one of all!

1. What does the speaker of the poem think of himself?_____

_____

_____

2. Write some advice for the boy who is speaking in the poem.

_____

_____

3. What would be a good title for this poem? _____

_____

Name _____

doctor

teacher

The endings *er* and *or* can sometimes show the job a person does. Write the job name below next to its description.

shipper	farmer	painter	pitcher
plumber	seller	doctor	sculptor
actor	teacher	donor	writer

1. a person who fixes plumbing _____

2. a person who makes sculptures _____

3. a person who donates something _____

4. a person who acts _____

5. a person who ships things _____

6. a person who farms _____

7. a person who pitches baseballs _____

8. a person who writes _____

9. a person who cares for other people's health _____

10. a person who paints things _____

11. a person who teaches _____

12. a person who sells things _____

Write the word that best completes each sentence.

> writer   actor   farmer
> painter   sculptor   plumber
> doctor   officer   speaker   teacher

It's fun to think about the jobs I could have someday. I like to put things

together. Once I saw a _____ putting the pipes and drains in a

new house. I also like to make old things look new. I once saw a

_____ make an old house look great by putting fresh paint on it.

    I like music and the arts, too. I love to put my hands in clay and make

things from it, so I might become a _____ . I enjoy thinking up

new stories and writing them on paper. It might be fun to be a

_____ , and have people read my stories. I like to act stories

out, too. I wonder if I could be a movie or television _____ .

    Since I am good at growing things, I might become a

_____ . I like to help other people learn new things, so I might

make a good _____ . It would be exciting to be a police

_____ to help people stay safe. Or maybe I will become a

_____ and help people stay healthy.

    Since I have so many ideas about

jobs, maybe I'll spend more time

speaking with others about their jobs.

That's it—I'll become a famous

_____ !

Harcourt Brace School Publishers

Name _____

Write the words that will make each sentence tell about the picture.

younger	fastest	smartest
livelier	most beautiful	more colorful
more upset		

1	The girl on the left is _____ than the girl on the right.
2	I think Mr. Martinez is the _____ teacher in the school.
3	The baby that is crying is _____ than the other one.
4	The painting that Joanne is holding is _____ than the other painting.
5	This man is the _____ shipper at the factory.
6	Rosa is picking the _____ flowers to give to her grandmother.
7	The puppy on the left is _____ than the one on the right.

Phonics Practice Book

Review of Comparatives and Superlatives:
-er, -est, more, most. Agents: -or, -er

287

Harcourt Brace School Publishers

Name _____

The people in my family have the most interesting jobs. My mom is a doctor. She sees all kinds of patients. Some are older than she is. She also sees the youngest people in town—the babies. The people here tell us she is the most trusted doctor in town.

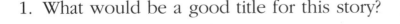

My dad is a famous sculptor. He gives art shows in our town and in the city. The shows in the city are bigger. My dad likes to speak with the people who come to look at his work. He is one of the liveliest speakers around. The people in our town go to his shows both here and in the city. They say my dad makes them feel famous, too, because he lives in their town.

I wonder what job I will have when I grow up. I might be a house painter, like my aunt. Or, I could be a symphony conductor, like Grandpa. Maybe my choice will be clearer to me when I get to middle school!

Harcourt Brace School Publishers

1. What would be a good title for this story?

   _____

2. What do the people in the town say about their doctor?

   _____

3. What does the storyteller say about deciding what job to have?

   _____

Now underline the words in the story that compare. Circle the words that tell what kind of job a person has.

Write the word from the box that completes each sentence.

slowly	sugarless	farmer	impossible
editor	nonsense	painter	portable
most	cheerful		

1. The turtle moved along _____.

2. Sheri always has a smile and a _____ word for everyone.

3. We watched the _____ mix the colors and get the brushes ready.

4. The _____ checked the writer's spelling.

5. I like silly cartoons, comic strips, and other _____.

6. My dentist says to try to eat _____ snacks for healthy teeth.

7. My mom says that few things are _____ if you try your hardest.

8. We have a _____ crib for my baby sister to use when we go places.

9. That surprise party was the _____ thoughtful thing anyone has ever done for me.

10. Todd's uncle is a _____ in Texas.

Write the word that matches the definition.

| washable | rewrite | actor | thankful |
| improper | prepay | disappear | unsafe |

1. able to be washed   _____

2. full of thanks   _____

3. the opposite of *appear*   _____

4. to pay before getting something   _____

5. not safe   _____

6. not proper   _____

7. to write again   _____

8. a person who acts   _____

Write the word that completes each sentence.

| deepest | sharper | more | most |

9. The river is at its _____ just before the waterfall.

10. My blue pencil is _____ than my yellow one.

11. This is the _____ beautiful flower I have ever seen.

12. Chocolate ice cream is _____ popular than strawberry.

Harcourt Brace School Publishers

Cumulative Review of Prefixes, Suffixes, Comparatives and Superlatives, and Agents

Phonics Practice Book

Name _____

Fill in the circle next to the word that best completes each sentence. Then write the word.

1	The _____ of this picture is my brother Frank.	○ plumber ○ painter ○ farmer
2	Mandy _____ peas.	○ dislikes ○ unlike ○ likely
3	We talked to our _____ after class.	○ donor ○ plumber ○ teacher
4	Marc watched a movie _____ .	○ viewable ○ viewer ○ preview
5	Pearls are of _____ value than pebbles.	○ greater ○ greatest ○ great
6	Our _____ plane made no stops at all.	○ stoppable ○ stops ○ nonstop
7	Do you know where the _____ place on Earth is?	○ cold ○ colder ○ coldest
8	Josh puts only _____ clothes into the washer.	○ rewash ○ wash ○ washable
9	Amy thinks soccer is _____ fun than basketball.	○ most ○ more ○ not

Harcourt Brace School Publishers

I love to hear Grandma retell stories she heard when she was young. Some things are impossible to believe, but they are fun to hear anyway. Grandma's stories are full of interesting people who do silly things. I don't think Grandma would really say anything untrue, but sometimes she stretches things a little bit.

Grandma is a wonderful storyteller. As she speaks, she changes her voice to sound like different people. And she comes up with the most remarkable props. She can quickly fold a piece of paper to become a ship or a hat— whatever her story needs.

Most of Grandma's stories don't seem preplanned. I think she just makes them up as she goes along. The saddest part of the day at Grandma's is when she has to discontinue the storytelling and I have to go to bed!

1 What would be a good title for this story?	○ Grandma's Special Stories ○ The Darkest Night ○ When the Writer Preplans
2 What must be true if Grandma's stories are *not* preplanned?	○ Grandma plans them ahead of time. ○ Grandma makes them up as she goes along. ○ She writes them down before she tells them.
3 What is the saddest part of the day at Grandma's?	○ when she calls the children in for supper ○ when she goes to work ○ when she discontinues the storytelling

Harcourt Brace School Publishers

Prefixes, Suffixes, Comparatives and Superlatives, and Word Endings Test

Phonics Practice Book

Before School

Before school, Jed gets the eggs after he has fed the hens. Then he takes the eggs back to his dad.

3

Fold

Harcourt Brace School Publishers

Now it's your turn! Tell and show something you do before school.

8

Fold

Before school, Meg takes Rags out for as long as she can. Then Rags does not feel so sad when Meg is at school.

6

Good Morning! It's time to get up.
There are things to do before school,
so get out of bed right now!

— Fold —

Before school, Nan lets her pet cat sit
on her lap for a while. Then the cat
might not feel so alone all day.

— Fold —

Before school, Pat helps her mother get
set to go to work. Mother likes to say,
"Pat, you are the best yet!"

Harcourt Brace School Publishers

7

Before school, Ben helps the others
get something to eat. Then he puts the
jams, cans, and bags away.

5

294

Cut-Out Fold-Up Book 1 • Short Vowels: *a, e*

Directions: Help your child cut and fold the book.

Getting Rid of Fox

"I'm keeping away from Fox," said Hen. "He comes around my hut a lot these days. I'm a bit afraid of him."

— Fold —

— Fold —

Harcourt Brace School Publishers

"You are the BEST!" said Hen. She gave them all a hug and a kiss. What do you think Hen will do next?

8

Buzz! Down came the flying Bat! Pop! Up jumped the big Dog. Zip! Out came Duck, nipping at Fox!

9

Directions: Help your child cut and fold the book.

Cut-Out Fold-Up Book 2 • Short Vowels: *i, o, u*

295

4

Hen sat on
top of her hut.
Dog, Duck, and
Bat came up.
"Why are you up
there, Hen?"
they asked.

2

"The next time you see
Fox, ask him in,"
said Dog. "We'll fix
him! We'll help
you get rid of Fox
for good."

"Help!" Fox ran
away, huffing and
puffing.
He never came
back. Bat, Dog, and
Duck got rid
of Fox for good.

7

Later, Hen said, "Come in, Fox!"
Fox licked his lips. He was thinking,
"At last, I'm in luck!"

5

Harcourt Brace School Publishers

Cut-Out Fold-Up Book 2 • Short Vowels: *i, o, u*

Directions: Help your child cut and fold the book.

Fold

Fold

Jean's Painting

Miss Clay said, "Go out and take a peek. Then, in painting class, you can sketch and paint what you have seen."

— Fold —

— Fold —

Harcourt Brace School Publishers

Here is Jean's painting. This time, no one asked, "What is it?" How do you think Jean feels now? Why?

"Wait," said Dave. "Why can't you take some real leaves? You could paste the leaves on your sheet and then —"

8

6

Directions: Help your child cut and fold the book.

Cut-Out Fold-Up Book 3 • Long Vowels: *a, e*

It was a very pretty day. Outside, the leaves on the trees were turning from green to red.

When they were outside, Jean wailed, "I hate painting class!"

"Why? What do you mean?" said Dave.

Fold

Fold

Harcourt Brace School Publishers

"Yes!" said Jean. "I could show a tree branch with leaves. I think I could sketch the branch, at least."

Jean said, "My paintings never look right. When I did one of a sheep last week, everyone said, 'What is it?'"

298

Cut-Out Fold-Up Book 3 • Long Vowels: *a, e*

Directions: Help your child cut and fold the book.

Livin' Limes

These nine green limes who loved to gloat,
Boasted every day in their home by a boat.

---Fold---

Harcourt Brace School Publishers

You see those nine sliced limes made a beautiful pie.
"Won't you have a slice? Come on, give it a try."

8

"We're nine huge limes, so full of pride.
Our rind is so beautiful, why should we hide?"

6

Directions: Help your child cut and fold the book.

Cut-Out Fold-Up Book 4 • Long Vowels: *i, o, u*

"We're nine cute limes, watch us grow.
We're ripe and fat, don't you know?"

Here are nine little limes sitting in a tree,
Soaking up the sun and humming with the bees.

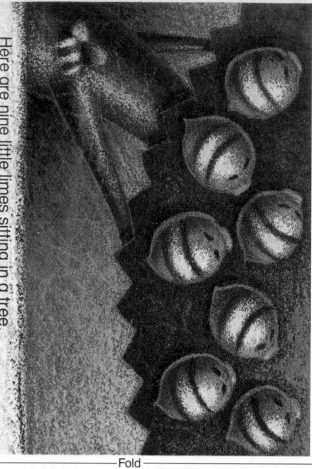

Fold ———————— Fold

So those nine silly limes, they laughed all day.
Even the bugs and the birds all ran away.

Then those nine plump limes began to cry
When a man from the boat came to spy.

Cut-Out Fold-Up Book 4 • Long Vowels: *i, o, u*

Directions: Help your child cut and fold the book.

CARP

They like to slurp insects and worms from rivers. Their strong tails swish back and forth in the ferns and grass.

3

Harcourt Brace School Publishers

When the wind blows, it looks like the carp are swimming hard—just like they do in the water.

8

In Japan, carp are very important because they have energy and power. Some people keep carp in their gardens. The carp may be orange, white, and black.

9

Directions: Help your child cut and fold the book.

Phonics Practice Book

Cut-Out Fold-Up Book 5 • R-Controlled Vowels

Some carp live on fish farms and become quite large—nearly three feet long!

Have you ever seen a carp in a pond? Carp are harmless fish that like to live in warm water.

2

4

— Fold —

— Fold —

Caring for carp is a lot of work. They need clear water, but many of them survive in dirty rivers.

5

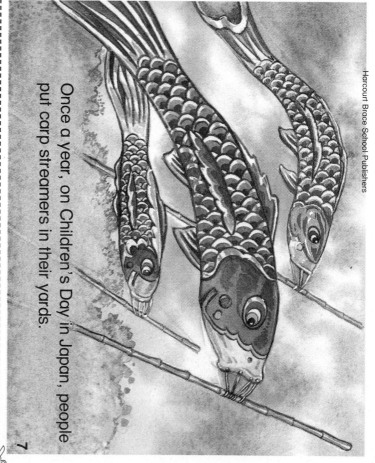

Once a year, on Children's Day in Japan, people put carp streamers in their yards.

7

Harcourt Brace School Publishers

302

Cut-Out Fold-Up Book 5 • R-Controlled Vowels

Directions: Help your child cut and fold the book.
Phonics Practice Book

Bitty Bloom's Mood

Her friends' laughter didn't change her mood. "Cheer up, Bitty. Have some food," said Drew.

Draw a picture to show what you think Bitty Bloom did.

"That gives me an idea," Bitty thought. "I know what would work!"

3

8

9

"Don't be blue, Bitty," said Floyd. "Let's give Bitty our Noisy Cheer," they said.

Bitty Bloom was a clown with a problem. She could not stop frowning.

Fold

Fold

"Turn around! Touch the ground! Walk on your hands! Make them laugh! Make them howl! Sing with the band!"

Bitty found her costume and props. "This will change my mood."

Harcourt Brace School Publishers

Cut-Out Fold-Up Book 6 • Vowel Diphthongs and Vowel Variants

Directions: Help your child cut and fold the book.

Phonics Practice Book